A must-read book for every man who  faithful and finish well. Jerry masterful navigating life dangers. Rooted in bibli .... discovered through a lifetime of walking closely with the Lord.

MARVIN CAMPBELL, US president of The Navigators

This is a survival playbook every man should have on hand. Like a trusted coach, Jerry exposes the often-unspoken perils capable of sidelining us during any season of our lives. His tactical advice—based on biblical truths and years of experience and illustrated by powerful personal stories—will give you steps you can take now to live a life of impact for God's Kingdom. Every one of us is vulnerable. But every one of us is also capable of yielding to the Holy Spirit and discovering the power of a life lived to its fullest.

EDGAR SANDOVAL SR, CEO and president of World Vision US

Jerry White gets into the minds of men. He writes like a friend. He understands like a brother.

LEITH ANDERSON, pastor; member of The Navigators board of directors; president emeritus of the National Association of Evangelicals

Grounded in Scripture and in decades of ministry experience, Jerry provides practical wisdom and a guide map for men who want to start and finish well with Jesus. He outlines the destinations for spiritual flourishing as well as the stop signs and detours we encounter along the way. In a culture where men grapple with identity, fear, and temptation perhaps more than any previous generation, this book is crucial for our discipleship.

TOM LIN, president and CEO of InterVarsity Christian Fellowship

Several things touch me about Jerry White's *Dangers Men Face*. First, he shares authentically from his own journey! No arrogant pontificating here—just a brother walking alongside us all. Jerry also takes a deep, comprehensive dive into so many areas of struggle specific to a man's life and masterfully connects specific biblical texts to each theme. Finally, and most importantly, sprinkled throughout is a compelling invitation to allow our healing and obedience to flow from our intimate love relationship with Jesus. Thanks, Jerry, for caring about us as brothers and pouring out your heart and years of wisdom on our behalf!

J. KEVIN BUTCHER, executive director of Rooted Ministries and author of *Choose and Choose Again* and *Free*

Jerry has blazed a path for men who want to live with purpose and fewer regrets. Honest, intimate, and filled with godly wisdom, this book is Jerry's legacy.

VINH CHUNG, MD, Fulbright Scholar and author of *Where the Wind Leads*

I know of no one better qualified to speak on crucial men's issues than Jerry White. His years of experience working with men regarding issues they face is invaluable! The ability to change society hinges on influencing men's worldview and spiritual awareness. These affect a man's ability to sustain relationships in the marketplace and, most importantly, in the home. Jerry writes with the smell of battle smoke due to his personal experiences. *Dangers Men Face* is an excellent resource for men, individually or in small-group discussions. Get it, use it, and see God work in the lives of men.

LAUREN LIBBY, international president/CEO of TWR International

Jerry is a spiritual leader who has lived life to the full. When he speaks on loss, danger, and sin, he writes as one who has been there and experienced the pain and joy of life. These aren't empty platitudes but the real wisdom of a man who has lived what he's teaching.

KEN HARRISON, CEO of Promise Keepers

In this twenty-fifth-anniversary edition, Jerry White brings us the fullness of who he is to help us think through and navigate life as men. The dangers we face in life have not changed much through the ages, but with each passing generation, they take on new dimensions. This anniversary edition is filled with new stories, godly wisdom, and instructive Scripture for navigating the dangers that confront us. This is a book all men should read, regardless of your age or whether you have read the first edition.

DG ELMORE, chairman of The Navigators Board

Jerry has been a mentor and friend for all my adult life. His vulnerability and wisdom have shown me how to navigate the balance between the exhilaration of an active life and its inherent dangers. If you are an honest man, you know already that unexpected and unseen dangers can lead to disaster for the unprepared. *Dangers Men Face* will prepare you for the obvious and the hidden dangers ahead. By all means, embrace the excitement of this life you've been given; but please join the company of the wise by using this book to open your eyes and prepare you for what lies ahead.

CHRIS CANLIS, owner of Canlis restaurant

Every pilot knows that it is dangerous to fly through a thunderstorm, or in icing conditions, or to attempt to land in dense fog. They are not born knowing these dangers. The dangers must be taught to them lest they learn through death-defying experience. The same holds true for the dangers men face in their daily flight through life, and Jerry White, in his straightforward and compelling writing style, has authored the primer that, if taken to heart, can help one avoid the many death-defying spiritual experiences we men face.

GENERAL KEVIN CHILTON, USAF, retired, astronaut

A powerful book that provides relevant and meaningful antidotes to navigate successfully through "five critical areas of danger that *every man* will face"—loss, sin, freezing, confusion, and withdrawal. In addition to helping readers spot and avoid unwise decisions that could maim or destroy a marriage or reputation, the book equips readers to finish life well in the "fourth quarter" by providing the ingredients to renew both the inner and outer man.

GREG STEPHENS, attorney and author of *Created for Greatness*

When Jerry started revising *Dangers Men Face*, I asked him to include a new chapter about one's identity in the fourth quarter of life (after age sixty). Most of our activity in life focuses on the first three quarters. But what's the role of identity in a Christian's fourth-quarter game plan? Being a follower of Jesus doesn't shield us from the challenges awaiting us in the fourth quarter. Are we relying on our résumé virtues of the first three quarters to carry us through the fourth? Or are we strengthening the character virtues that are emphasized at our eulogy? Jerry addresses these critical questions and many more, including: Does a Christian's game plan change in the fourth quarter—and is it more offensive or defensive? How do unexpected challenges and our changing physical abilities in the fourth quarter affect our identity and our game plan? This revised edition is a must-read, shedding new light on how we think about identity in the fourth quarter.

DR. TERRY PIERCE, captain, USN, retired; former director of the Center of Innovation at the United States Air Force Academy; author of *Without Warning: The Saga of Gettysburg*; former speechwriter for the Chief of Naval Operations

OVERCOMING

THE GREATEST THREATS

DANGERS
MEN FACE

TO LIVING LIFE

WELL

JERRY WHITE

NavPress

A NavPress resource published in alliance
with Tyndale House Publishers

NavPress is the publishing ministry of The Navigators, an international Christian organization and leader in personal spiritual development. NavPress is committed to helping people grow spiritually and enjoy lives of meaning and hope through personal and group resources that are biblically rooted, culturally relevant, and highly practical.

For more information, visit NavPress.com.

To the memory of our son
Stephen Jerry White
(1959–1990)

His life and his death have caused me to reflect more deeply
on all the dangers described in this book.

Contents

About This Revised Edition

Everything changes but change itself.
Everything flows and nothing remains the same.
You cannot step twice into the same river,
for other waters and yet others go flowing ever on.

HERACLITUS OF EPHESUS
(FIFTH-CENTURY GREEK PHILOSOPHER)

WHAT HAS CHANGED since the initial writing of this book?

Very little, and yet so much.

My friends and counselors affirm that the essential dangers remain the same. However, our culture has steadily changed. "For the worse," the cynic would say. While those in their twenties and thirties would simply say, "This is normal"—having little sense that it has degraded or improved.

Even if I were to evaluate our culture, my assessment would be only the perception of an American in a Western culture. Every country and culture undergo change and transformation over the decades. Some decline and are even destroyed; others are rebuilt. In the midst of all this, the dangers I describe in this book still permeate the lives of men of every decade, modified only by technological and communication changes of enormous magnitude. Our virtual society allows for few secrets. We know and see more—yet our passions, feelings, desires, and fears remain much the same.

The origins of this book were my puzzling over the mysterious responses and reactions of men in our international Navigator context. I still have a crumpled piece of paper on which I wrote notes about some of these dangers. I wrestled with the struggles I saw in many of my friends. I soon realized they were the same dangers I faced. I was not immune. I wasn't the wise analyst shrewdly looking at the foibles of others. No, I could see the problem, and it was me.

There's no finger-pointing. As men, we're in this together.

The birth of this book was complicated even more by the sudden and untimely death of my son. This drained my emotional strength to such an extent that my energy and motivation for writing were often squeezed out by my work demands as the international president of The Navigators, as well as by the incessant changes taking place in my own life and that of my family.

I turned to friends to clarify my thinking. The men in our covenant group—Doug Hignell, Chris Canlis, and Stan Newell—kept me accountable in the many areas mentioned in this writing.

My wife, Mary, continued to encourage and edit even as she worked on her book *Harsh Grief, Gentle Hope*. Mary has been my collaborator and friend through years of marriage, suffering, and leadership. Although I address men, Mary sees similar patterns for women.

For this updated and revised edition, many men made significant suggestions. My grandson Jerad Birch helped with the perspective of his generation. Excellent suggestions for this revision also came from Captain (USN, Retired) Terry Pierce, General (USAF, Retired) Kevin Chilton, Colonel (USAF, Retired) Lee Hall, and attorney Greg Stephens, as well as others.

Through the years, as I've taught this material, many other people have offered important insights and ideas. And I've added here a significant chapter on life's "fourth quarter."

The illustrations are real, though some are composites and altered for privacy. I've used actual names of people only with their permission.

The ideas and principles here are not theoretical. They are real, having been forged in the crucible of my own life and the lives of many friends, and molded by Scripture.

The accompanying Bible study and discussion guide will help you delve more personally into a better understanding of what you discover here and will help you apply the ideas and principles to your own life.

Navigate these dangers with me.

Jerry White
Colorado Springs
APRIL 2022

DANGEROUS JOURNEY, EXCITING JOURNEY

NO MAN SETS OUT EARLY in his life to destroy himself. He doesn't plan to foster failure after failure. He doesn't get married intending to make himself and his wife miserable. He doesn't plan to be a poor father. He doesn't coldly calculate how he'll become an alcoholic and ruin his liver by age forty.

But the journey is filled with danger. And finishing well is a tremendous challenge.

At the beginning, a man envisions a life of fulfillment and at least moderate success. Maybe he dreams of a lovely wife and family living in a comfortable home. Perhaps he plans to take his daughter to gymnastics and his son to Little League baseball. He imagines a stable job and financial success. He sees himself happily walking his daughter down the aisle at her wedding. He envisions playing with his grandchildren and spoiling them on birthdays and holidays.

Even though the expectations of many young people today may be different from the aspirations of previous generations, young people today still want to create a compelling future. They may delay marriage and change jobs more freely and frequently. But they still search for special experiences and experiment to ultimately arrive at their careers and find fulfillment in life.

Few men write out these dreams. But they're there, as present as the sunrise, as compelling as a smile from a beautiful woman—especially the one he hopes will be his wife. Dreams are often unspoken, but they're always present in the recesses of his mind. Just as a young boy might fantasize about being a star pro football player or baseball player, so every man fantasizes about his future.

A boy's picture of his future gradually evolves as he grows up. He observes his father's foibles as well as his successes. Or he sees many fathers in the serial marriage scene. His idealistic picture develops a few cracks. He doesn't want to be like that. He sees role models in teachers, neighbors, coaches. Most young men have little discernment as to the quality of these role models. But something inside picks the best of them all and creates the dream—absent of trouble and full of happiness.

A friend recently sent me a picture taken when I was eleven. There I am, a blond, smiling, shy young boy who had no idea what was ahead. I remember even at that innocent age the fears had begun that life wasn't all it was cracked up to be. Yet my life was an empty page waiting for a story to be written.

As a young man embarks on the teen years and young adulthood, the cold reality of life begins to sober him. The idyllic road is not so smooth after all. There are bumps and potholes, detours and dead ends, hills and valleys. It's a road filled with dangers at every turn—some under our control, but many coming upon us like a sudden afternoon thunderstorm.

The word *danger* brings a variety of mental pictures, depending on a man's experience. Some men remember a near collision at an intersection while driving. One may remember escaping a terrible accident with only minor injuries, despite having totally wrecked his car. Others think of children playing too close to a precipice or near a busy street. Some recall a child not coming home from school on time, causing a frantic search and the fear of abduction. Some may recall terrifying incidents of abuse and mistreatment. Others fear having no money or job.

But with danger comes great opportunity. There is risk, but there is also much gain in navigating an exciting life. It's a challenge we should look forward to, not a journey we should walk in fear.

Each of the dangers mentioned above are real. Any one of them could happen. But the dangers we need to fear most are the ones we don't see until it's too late. It's like one occasion when I visited a country where the cars drive on the left side of the road. As a pedestrian, I instinctually wanted to look in the wrong direction for traffic. Once when I did this and was about to cross the street, I was suddenly restrained by a friend who knew I would make that mistake. He protected me from getting hit.

Danger is like a cancer that grows within us, unknown until it sinks roots of death into our bodies.

Danger is like the cholesterol clogging our arteries, building silently until we have a heart attack.

In the next handful of chapters, it's the unexpected and unseen dangers—those that are silent and subtle—that I'll address. They're spiritual and practical dangers that I believe every man faces almost daily—but they're so silent that they often slide by unnoticed. The effects of these dangers dull our spiritual lives, cripple our effectiveness and happiness, and generally turn us away from a vital walk with God. And as a natural corollary, they poison a man's relationships with his wife, children, and friends.

Even for a committed believer in Christ, these dangers are always present. It's not just casual believers or half-hearted believers who are at risk. Most of us believe that "the devil prowls around like a roaring lion looking for someone to devour" (1 Peter 5:8). But this truth is more sinister than it may appear, and I would expand and paraphrase the passage this way: "Satan sneaks about seeking whom he can entice and coax into the first delicious steps of seemingly harmless indiscretion."

In the upcoming short chapters, I will share from my experience—and from the Scriptures—some particular dangers that have the potential to destroy a man, just as cancer destroys the body. These dangers vary from subtle to blatant, avoidable to unavoidable, constant to intermittent. I've seen these primary dangers in my own life and in the lives of others. A great danger for one man may be a minor one for another. We're all different and respond differently to circumstances and events. But to some extent, we face all these dangers at some point in our lives.

It would be totally unfair to simply throw up danger signs without telling you where to turn—instructions on how to either drive carefully through the danger zone or take a detour around it. With each danger we'll look at, I'll identify one or two key biblical concepts as antidotes or preventives. Profound, fundamental truths undergird much of what I share. These truths include God's grace, God's sovereignty, the nature of salvation, the person and work of Christ, the pervasiveness of sin, the nature of humanity, and the place of good works. These are important biblical concepts that rightfully warrant far more than I can write here. In this book, I often refer to the basic tenets of life in Christ, but I leave it to you to pursue them further, depending on where you are in your spiritual pilgrimage.

Even with dangers, you can experience a great adventure. We don't just curl up and hide, never taking a risk.

Walk with me now through these danger zones. Embark on a great adventure.

PART ONE

Dangers of Loss

THE REALITY OF LOSS

EARLY ONE COLD JANUARY MORNING, when I was eight years old, I climbed into a car with my mother and my new stepfather. After seven years as a single mom, my mother was embarking on a new life, a new journey, leaving behind deep hurts from her divorce. We were leaving the tiny town of Garden City, Iowa, and heading to an unknown future in the state of Washington.

Before driving off, I said tearful good-byes. I was leaving behind my grandfather—the man who'd become my surrogate father following my parents' divorce, back when I was only a few months old. I loved Grandpa Tony dearly, depended on him, found my security in him. And now I was losing him—for what I thought was forever. Promises of letters don't mean much to an eight-year-old. And in that day and age, long-distance phone calls were virtually unheard of for ordinary people.

We settled in Spokane, Washington, a city of 180,000 people, and I found my new stepfather to be a gentle and fine person. But he was not Grandpa Tony. I became so lonely that my mother decided the only solution was to send me back to Iowa to visit. For several years, I made that trek each summer to be with my grandfather. He was a widower, so we "bached" together. I was trying to recover some of what I had lost.

Every human being must grapple with the reality of loss. From our earliest years, we experience the joys of gain and the agony of loss. Dealing with loss is one of the basic building blocks of maturity. Some of our losses are open wounds, clearly seen and painful. Others are silent, unknown except for their pervasive effects on our current and later lives. How much did my parents' divorce affect me? At the time, I sensed no emotional loss, since I was only a baby when it happened. Yet it was a real loss with real consequences, and thousands of children growing up with only one parent feel that same void. Certainly, for my mother, the divorce affected her emotional state for many years to come, thus also influencing me in countless subtle ways.

In retrospect, I can more fully understand her anxieties and responses in our home and family. My mother and stepfather had a wonderful relationship, but they faced struggles in adjusting, especially with the clear evidence of the previous marriage always there in the form of my presence. It could not have been easy for them. Even in adulthood, I didn't inquire into this aspect of their lives. It seemed too private, too sensitive to discuss.

For me, living seven years without a father and then gaining a new stepfather certainly created both wounds and strengths. The classic father-son bond never developed between my stepfather and me. There were many struggles as I exerted my independence, not unlike any teenager. Some of the normal fatherly discipline was absent. I don't remember ever being disciplined by my stepfather; perhaps he never felt he had the right. Would I have been more securely attached to my natural father? Would I have had a different childhood? Certainly. But I can't say it would have been better or healthier. The loss was history—and I had to make the best of it.

In sports, the opposite of a loss is a win. In life, losing and winning are more complicated. From our earliest days, we're taught the joy and importance of winning. Our youth are inculcated with the idea that it's imperative to win—in sports, arguments, war, board games, and life in general.

Some in our culture downplay competition and winning. That's an interesting philosophy, but one that's rarely understood or embraced by young men. In fact, we applaud when our children win a game, make a shot, get a hit, score a goal, or star in a drama at school. We comfort them when they fail. We watch their emotions soar and sink. The not-so-subtle message is that it's good to win and bad to lose. We may try to teach them to be good sports (that is, good losers), and we may deeply believe that's important. But we also communicate that it's better to win.

I've played many games with my grandchildren. When they were young, I could easily win. If they won, they were elated; they laughed and clapped. They loved to beat me! If I won, they soberly asked for another game. Right there, they were learning to cope with loss and compare the joys of winning and the sorrows of losing. But inside, they still had a deep desire to win.

In real life, what comprises winning and losing is less clear.

We want our children to be winners in life. We want to build their self-esteem. We want them to be confident. We also want them to know how to handle defeat, since not everyone can be a winner in every contest.

In life, every man will face critical issues of loss that will either build his character or destroy his will to keep growing as a man. In life, the scorecard is elusive.

We face many losses in life: death, disappointment, and the loss of jobs, money, or relationships. Several primary losses deeply affect men, sneaking up on them and subtly endangering their well-being. These include loss of motivation, loss of position, loss of influence, loss of identity, and loss of confidence. There are certainly other types of losses, but these represent the primary ones I've observed and researched. These losses strike deeply at a man's ego and being. To a great extent, they're inevitable. It's just a matter of time until one or more of these losses challenge *your* life—and place you in danger. They're what I call the "predictable losses" of life. Though predictable, they nevertheless usually surprise us, catching us unprepared.

Over the next several chapters, we'll look at these predictable losses in more depth.

3

LOSS OF MOTIVATION

MAJOR JACK WYMAN was a dedicated and hardworking Air Force officer. After leaving one of the best military assignments, he was assigned to a job outside the country. He performed superbly. However, the officer who wrote his performance review was in the United States and didn't really know Jack personally. "Out of sight, out of mind" governed his rating. He did not give Jack the top rating. Although this was disappointing for Jack, it wasn't the end of the world.

The promotion board met to select people for lieutenant colonel. When the list came out, Jack did not receive a call of congratulations from his commander. The silence was deafening.

The next day the list was published. Jack's name was not on it. He'd been passed over. He knew his career was destroyed.

After learning this, Jack didn't want to talk to anyone. He was embarrassed and crushed. His appetite for work diminished. Getting up to go to work was a chore. He could no longer do it.

Jack Wyman had lost his motivation.

Sociologists and business researchers have tried for decades to define *motivation*. They've studied human behavior and tried to learn how to motivate people. Psychologists and psychiatrists deal daily with people who've lost their motivation and have become seriously depressed. Hundreds of books have been written to help a person move toward self-motivation. The recommended solutions range from manipulative self-actualization to the accumulation of wealth. Some self-help authors recount personal success experiences, while others just offer plain hype designed to sell a book.

Motivation is what gives someone a compelling reason for doing something. It's what makes us eager to do, to act, to accomplish. But that definition may not help you much, since motivation is something you sense or feel emotionally.

Motivational books and online podcasts and seminars abound, all to help us be motivated. And most men want to be motivated. They don't want to move through life only doggedly surviving, with no real joy in living and working.

Before we can recover or increase our motivation, we must ask, "Motivation for what?" Each activity needs its own motivation—to work, to eat, to read, to learn, to exercise, to get out of bed, or to help someone in need. At times, obligation and motivation become confused. We do some things simply because we must do them to survive. We do other tasks from a deep inner desire or drive.

Motivation is one of the most intangible qualities. We possess individual personalities, needs, backgrounds, experiences, and intellects. No one formula will motivate all of us. And sometimes we despair that nothing will work.

It Affects Every Man

Motivational loss is frightening, especially for men who are used to being positive and excited about life. Every man will eventually suffer moderate to severe loss of motivation. When it happens, we become confused. We recognize it, but we feel powerless to change our feelings.

Stephanie Hertzenberg comments, "Everyone loses motivation at some point. You get tired, you get discouraged or you just run out of willpower. In those moments, it can be easy to give up."[1]

I've seen students who've lost all motivation for going to class. Some would skip classes and sleep all day, staying awake all night. They were either fearful or couldn't see how their studies would benefit them. Finally, they would flunk out of school.

When we lack motivation, there is a sense of purposelessness, a lack of drive, a feeling that nothing matters. An inability to act takes over. Critical tasks remain undone. Going to work is drudgery. And all this spills over into family life, causing conflicts and misunderstandings. It can debilitate us spiritually and even lead to moral failure.

Causes of Motivational Loss

What causes this precipitous decrease in motivation? Many things may trigger it: the loss of a job, perceived or real failure, marriage problems, illness, fatigue, stress, age, or boredom.

I've experienced various swings in motivation over the years. In 1990, a severe loss threw me into a lingering period when my motivation stayed at a low ebb. In April of 1990, my thirty-year-old son was brutally murdered while working at one of his two jobs. He had his own broadcast on a local public radio station, and he drove his own taxi to put bread on the table. But one night a customer set out simply to kill someone. And that someone who answered the call for a taxi was my son.

Shock and grief overwhelmed our lives for months. Before this tragic event, much of my motivational being was consumed by leading The Navigators and helping people grow spiritually. It was a tremendous challenge. But after Steve's death, it seemed that nothing mattered anymore. His death put every activity of my life in a different perspective. My life went on hold. Even spiritual activities seemed trivial and inconsequential. I wondered if purpose and motivation would ever return.

Weeks and months went by as I continued in my leadership tasks, knowing that I wasn't "all there." People were very patient and understanding. My motivation came back slowly as I recovered from grief.

Motivation returned but in a very different form. Position and responsibility mattered little. A purifying and cleansing had taken place in my soul. I viewed life—and death—differently. I spent much time wrestling with critical biblical issues—God's sovereignty, God's goodness, prayer—and all those puzzling "whys" of life. (My wife, Mary, has written extensively about this time of our lives in her book *Harsh Grief, Gentle Hope*.) [2]

Clearly, this loss of motivation resulted from a tragic event.

I experienced another time of decreased motivation when I sensed I wasn't doing a good job in my leadership and received strong criticism.

Usually, there's some event that triggers such a loss. Even the apostle Paul experienced this loss of motivation, alluding to his own depression: "For even when we came into Macedonia our flesh had no rest, but we were afflicted on every side: conflicts without, fears within. But God, who comforts the depressed, comforted us by the coming of Titus" (2 Corinthians 7:5-6, NASB).

I can relate to that. Conflicts, problems, and pressures are all around. Fears and turmoil capture mind and soul. And in the midst of the havoc, motivation disappears. Trying to identify the reasons may help, but the conflicts and fears remain just the same.

Many paths lead to a loss of motivation. Personality is a factor. So is a person's age and stage of life. Life traumas contribute. Failing health exacerbates the problem. Sometimes we call it "burnout." We despise the feelings and silently cry out to be rescued.

But that's the problem: The cry is often silent.

Men find it so difficult to call for help. We go on and suffer in silence rather than admit the weakness we've seen in ourselves. *After all, what will people think? I'll lose respect. I may lose my job. I'll just gut it out. It'll go away.*

Sometimes it does go away. But then the deeper issues of our lives rumble inwardly, unheard and unmet. Some of these issues stem from our more evil side—love of money, love of power, desire for comfort and material possessions, abuse of authority, domination of people. Other issues arise out of our insecurities. *Am I liked? Do people respect me? What if I don't achieve my potential? What if I fail?*

Biblical Solutions and Basic Motivations

The topic of motivation has been studied extensively, especially as it relates to workers and productivity. Much has been written on self-motivation and managerial motivation. (One of my favorite studies is *Working* by Studs Terkel.)[3] For the past several years, I've studied motivation to discover biblical solutions. I've found that most secular motivational techniques are manipulative and coercive, and the Christian counterparts are largely warmed-over secular ideas with some spiritual vocabulary and a few verses. Even today, I'm not prepared to write a full book on the subject. I know there are deep roots of motivation that go beyond the surface psychological indicators that we all experience.

Basic motivations find roots in desire (lust), fear, and love.

We're motivated to do some things out of a great desire—to make money, achieve education, be promoted, get married, maintain a good marriage. As long as the desire remains strong, we remain motivated. When the desire wanes, our motivation disappears. And it will wane. Desire isn't ultimately the best foundation for motivation.

Fear is an incredibly effective motivator. It's a basic instrument of survival. Fear of losing a job, losing respect, losing a marriage, or failing often keeps us going. But fear as a basic motivation is short lived. It only works for a brief time before it eats at one's inner person and erupts in anger and rebellion.

The Greatest Motivator

The greatest of all motivators is *love*, though it's the least used or understood in our modern world. In spite of considerable teaching on relationships, people skills, values, and equality, we still fail to grasp the simple power of love.

Love of God. Love of people. Love of ourselves. Love of family. Each of these loves brings a dimension to motivation that makes desire and fear look weak. But love seems too simple an answer, too easily said. We need to know *how* to develop love as a basis for our motivation.

Desire and fear are counterfeits of love. Desire becomes lust, just as sexual love easily becomes lust. Fear is a replacement for love. "There is no fear in love; but perfect love casts out fear, because fear involves punishment" (1 John 4:18, NASB). We inflict fear or respond to fear when love is missing.

Appreciating and expressing love can be difficult for a man, yet it's key to motivation. For many men, the tendency is to show love by doing, not hugging. (There's helpful guidance on this in the books *Desiring God* by John Piper and *Love Does* by Bob Goff.)[4]

Natural Motivators

Before leaving this discussion, let's ask: Are desire and fear illegitimate motivators?

Not entirely. Desire is a natural human drive—for food and nourishment, for love and security, for pleasure and comfort. When desire has a root in God and His Word, it becomes holy. Desire relates to the longings of our hearts. These longings are placed within us by God.

Men often find it difficult to express the deepest longings of their hearts. These are longings for things only God can fully supply—longings to be holy, to do good, to be a man of integrity, to be respected, and to be used by God. We've tasted these longings, but most often we've had just a taste. We need a feast. Then we'll experience real motivation from desire.

Fear is also a legitimate motivator as long as it's properly focused. "Fear God and keep his commandments" (Ecclesiastes 12:13); "The fear of the LORD is the beginning of wisdom" (Proverbs 9:10).

God is to be feared because He alone has the true power of judgment. We can be secure in His love, as children are secure in their father's love. Children have a healthy fear of their father, and this leads to obedience and doing what is right. We need that motivation. But fear is a legitimate motivator only in relation to God, not to other people.

Overcoming Motivational Fears

Let me give you the rest of the story of Air Force Major Jack Wyman. After he was passed over for promotion, he began to think—and to pray. *Wasn't God sovereign? Was this the worst thing that could happen to him?* He began to see his entire career in a different light. He determined to continue working hard and to keep going. He found himself thanking God for the trial.

When he went on mandatory retirement as a major, he saw it as a great opportunity. He not only survived, but he regained his motivation, launching into a successful second career. He'd lost his fear of failure.

Inevitably, our motivation will wane or even disappear for a period of time. The danger is not so much the loss of motivation as it is how we respond to that loss. If God is the source of our life, then He will sustain us through every dampening of our human motivation.

As you read this book, let me encourage you to follow the leading of the Holy Spirit in the areas He points out to you. It's a matter of life and death—of spiritual survival.

Larry Crabb put it this way:

> Nothing matters more than developing a passion for Christ as we try to handle life's struggles responsibly and wisely. Our primary purpose is not to use God to solve problems but to move through our problems toward finding God.[5]

That's our overriding purpose—to know Christ more deeply and to follow Him with all our hearts. Remember the words of missionary martyr Jim Elliot: "He is no fool who gives what he cannot keep to gain that which he cannot lose."[6]

As we move through life, we constantly seek to be aligned with God's purpose for us. As we encounter trials, we're forced more deeply into examining and revising our most foundational purposes. It's all part of a refining fire that God uses to drive us to deeper dependence on Him.

Now we turn to the next loss, one that's often the source of a man's loss of motivation: his loss of position.

4

LOSS OF POSITION

POSITION DESCRIBES THE ROLES we hold in life—manager, foreman, designer, engineer, salesman, farmer, owner, supervisor, machine operator, deacon, elder, father, husband. The one common denominator of all positions is that they are temporary. With the exception of family roles, positions seldom last for a lifetime. Even family roles morph into different expressions of position.

I've talked with men who've lost their jobs. Pain fills their eyes. Their voices are dull. Nothing strikes at the ego of a man like being out of work. It reveals our great dependence on what we do for our sense of identity.

No matter how much we may believe we're above that kind of identification, we still inwardly depend on it. Our value, our drive, our personhood become inextricably intertwined with our work. Even the man who hates his job still receives much of his identity from it. "What do you do?" becomes a feared question when one no longer has a job or position.

One of my friends was removed from his managerial responsibilities. Later he lost his job. He expressed and shared his pain. He admitted it—and also hated his feelings and responses. He couldn't shake them off by simply admitting them. Inner feelings aren't always controlled by the mind or reason. Loss of position is like a small death.

This is not unique to men. Women, especially those in the workplace, face the same loss. All losses chip away at our loves and egos.

When a position dies, many areas of our lives are affected. We become more focused on money. *Is there enough? How do I get more?* Our marriages begin to show strain. Little conflicts with our wives become big conflicts. Our children begin to see a change in us as we turn our attention from them to ourselves. Even our friendships and our health suffer if we take this loss of position too seriously. But how else can a man take it?

One of the motivating factors in our work is a desire to solidify our positions. We work diligently to gain a higher position. Isn't that career progression? Fear of losing their positions drives many men to a cutthroat view of life at work. This is a dead-end road. At some point, we'll lose.

One businessman told me that at the end of each day he would call a friend and ask, "Did you draw any blood today?" Work was a form of war. Winning meant spilling blood. Losing position wasn't an option.

Loss also comes when a job is eliminated or disappears because of change, company downsizing, or lack of performance. In the work world, we'll all eventually lose our positions, through retirement or otherwise.

Loss of position occurs not only in the workplace but also in many other areas of life. Divorce robs us of the position of husband and erodes our ability to father. The egos of both men and women are severely damaged by the failure of a marriage. The loss devastates multiple victims. The loss of position at work fades in significance to the loss of divorce. Work may then become a new challenge to prove ourselves and counter the loss in the home.

Even in the church, we become position dependent. Elders, deacons, teachers, and committee members are all positions of responsibility that give a certain status in a congregation. Conflict, growth of the church, and growing older can precipitate a loss of a church position. Many men who have little recognition or position in the working world often turn to positions in the church. But if they are merely seeking recognition, this can be as harmful as overvaluing position. Meanwhile, a great contribution can be made when we view our positions in the church as opportunities to serve for God's glory.

What's the big deal about position? Why is it such an important thing to men?

From our earliest days as children, we're taught by parents, teachers, role models, and the media that title and position reflect success and accomplishment. Authority, respect, and honor are given to people of certain positions. It's a fact of society. In some parts of the world, different criteria are used for "positioning"—age, heritage, or education, for instance—but it's still there.

As early as the elementary school years, elections and selections take place—line leader, student of the week, class president, class secretary. These are excellent means of building self-esteem and confidence. I applaud them. But like so many good things, they communicate other messages that linger in our minds for a lifetime.

I'm not at all in favor of a classless society or of making no distinctions for ability and responsibility. But when one becomes an adult, new thinking needs to emerge. Achievement is important; success is important. Let's not downgrade it. But let's recognize the fact that it's inevitably temporary—and not the source of our identity or worth.

For several years in The Navigators, we've understood that in God's view, position is less important than function. We've tried to downplay titles and a hierarchical view of leadership and to emphasize teamwork and tasks. Yet human nature being what it is, people and organizations tend to invent or attach a scaled meaning to certain jobs. Men are insatiably position oriented.

The military is a classic example of this. It's an "up or out" system. To stay in the military, you must advance or get promoted. A clear hierarchy exists. We pay deference and salute.

In other professions, position and responsibility are connected. Accountability and authority allow a business to function well and make a profit. Many men are happy to remain in a subordinate role, while others constantly strive for promotion. An increase in pay accompanies an increase in position, which gives additional motivation.

So let's accept two realities. First, position is a fact of life—a necessary and useful fact of life. Second, every position is ultimately temporary and will disappear.

Maxing Out

In addition to losing position, there's the reality of maxing out—reaching the limit of our abilities or opportunities and being denied the next promotion. In the military, reaching the rank of full colonel is an honor achieved by about only 5 percent of all officers. One of my friends was not only a colonel but was selected to serve in a brigadier general position and to compete for that rank. However, he was not promoted. He suffered a blow to his ego. He nearly refused to have a retirement ceremony as a colonel. Yet if he hadn't had the opportunity for the next rank, he would have been thrilled to retire as a colonel.

This is common in many industries where promotions are limited. Both opportunity and ability play a role. This leads us to a further discussion of gaining a realistic view of ourselves. No one is omnicompetent. We each have limitations. These limitations are God-given in terms of our gifts and abilities.

All of us will lose our positions eventually. At some point, younger people or others more qualified than us will take our places, and we'll step aside. Loss of position is inevitable.

The Bible records many stories of men who lost their positions. The key insight into each man's character is how he reacted to his losses.

When God rejected Saul as Israel's first king, Saul fought tooth and nail to keep his position. He murdered, schemed, and blasphemed God in the process. Eventually he committed suicide by falling on his sword.

When David, Saul's successor, lost his position and was chased out of his palace, he understood that it may have occurred according to God's sovereign will.

Significant consequences result from a loss of position. Finances can be greatly reduced. Embarrassment certainly accompanies the loss. Public status changes significantly. People view a man differently. Anger, bitterness, and loss of self-esteem create inner turmoil. These reactions provide fertile ground for God to work deeply in a man's character.

Handling Positional Loss

Loss offers an opportunity to test character. Though painful, loss presents one of the greatest growth opportunities of life.

Mike had given his life to his company. He succeeded in almost everything he did. He was rewarded by promotion after promotion. Finally, he became president and chief executive officer of the company. He'd reached the pinnacle of his career. His first two years at the top were rocky but successful.

Then he made a series of bold, strategic moves that damaged the company financially. After several months of trying to pull the company through the difficulties, he was asked to resign. It was as though his entire life was being torn apart. Embarrassment and a sense of failure engulfed him.

He decided that this was God at work in his life. He graciously stepped aside, helping his successor get started. He was asked to lead a major division of the company. Quite a step down. Rather than allowing himself to become bitter or discouraged, Mike took the new position with energy and gusto. He gained respect within the company as people observed him overcome adversity and serve the company rather than himself.

Broader Understanding

What are the facts of position?

- Position is good and necessary in life and society.
- We place value on position.
- Every position is temporary.
- Loss of position is inevitable. Only the timing is in question.

When we understand these facts and bring them into perspective, we can more easily surrender our positions, realizing they don't define who we are. As we see position from God's viewpoint, we become free, allowing Him to use it, change it, or eliminate it.

Here's a passage that has helped me in this: "Promotion cometh neither from the east, nor from the west, nor from the south. But God is the judge: he putteth down one, and setteth up another" (Psalm 75:6-7, KJV).

Even when a man doesn't have a position, he may have something even more significant—personal influence. What happens, then, when we lose this influence? We'll look at that next.

5

LOSS OF INFLUENCE

HE SAT AT THE GATE TO THE CITY. An unusually handsome man, he was the son of the king. People were naturally drawn to him. He was the consummate politician, intercepting people coming to plead their cases for justice before the king. He lied, telling them they would not receive a hearing from the king but that he himself would gladly hear them—if only he were in a position of power.

"So Absalom stole away the hearts of the men of Israel" (2 Samuel 15:6, NASB). Absalom was a traitor to his father, King David, and soon staged a coup.

David fled Jerusalem for his life as his son approached the city. Ahithophel, who'd been a trusted counselor to David, joined the conspiracy. Ahithophel took on the role of chief counselor to Absalom in the new power structure. He seemed invincible in his counsel: "The advice of Ahithophel, which he gave in those days, was as if one inquired of the word of God; so was all the advice of Ahithophel regarded by both David and Absalom" (2 Samuel 16:23, NASB). Talk about influence! Ahithophel had it! He was riding the crest of his career.

Then something happened. David's adviser, Hushai, spoke to Absalom, convincing him to go against Ahithophel's counsel. What was Ahithophel's response?

> Now when Ahithophel saw that his counsel was not followed, he saddled his donkey and arose and went to his home, to his city, and set his house in order, and strangled himself.
>
> 2 SAMUEL 17:23, NASB

All because he lost his influence. A sad end to a stellar career. He demonstrated great error of judgment. His doom was sealed. He tragically compounded his error by reacting to his loss of influence in the king's court. He took the ultimate step of rejection—suicide.

The Nature of Influence

Not everyone can have a position of power or responsibility in our society like Ahithophel. But everyone does have influence. Each of us relishes making a difference or being influential in others' lives or in some small part of society.

We influence our children and grandchildren. We influence friends, coworkers, and other believers. In all likelihood, we're an expert in some skill or field. So people ask for our help and counsel.

Influence is pervasive and multifaceted. There's the influence of your *person*—who you are. Your personality, character, experience, age, and wisdom all make up who you are. You may never have held a great position, but people still come to you for advice. You may be a youth leader, an elder, or just a good listener. At work, you know the ropes, so new hires seek you out.

I know people in The Navigators who are not in the leadership structure because that's not their gift. But they're godly and wise. They have great insight and godly counsel. They have depth of character. They wield incredible influence. They're sought out for their godly wisdom and counsel. That's their gift.

There's also influence of *performance*. Some people are incredibly skilled and gifted in leadership: speaking, managing, organizing, strategizing, thinking, coordinating projects, getting things done, selling, analyzing, or otherwise employing their manual, technical, or mechanical skills. Their performance and track records open doors of influence. We regularly see top executives in successful corporations who get drawn to another company. They're sought after.

In every field of work, performance earns you the right to be heard. Often people's abilities lead them to positions of influence. Some influence comes from position, but even then, the influence of your person is important.

Through the years, I've met a number of top military leaders. I've recognized their true giftedness in leading and thinking. They attained their positions by their skilled performance over many years. One Air Force chief of staff (the senior uniformed officer in the Air Force) developed a set of values that are still in effect today: *Integrity first. Service before self. Excellence in all we do.*

I clearly recall, as a newly promoted brigadier general, a meeting of all new Air Force generals where the chief of staff announced: "If any of you are sleeping around with someone who isn't your spouse, you'd better stop it now, or you'll be found out and fired!" His position allowed him to speak that strongly with the force of authority.

Some people influence others through their *knowledge*. Through education and personal intellectual ability, they develop a reservoir of information, specialized knowledge, or analytical tools that pave the way for their influence. In politics and business, these individuals become special counselors and advisers. In the church body, they are theologians and thinkers who influence by their knowledge. Many leaders have put their knowledge into books that continue to influence people for decades. In the Christian realm, these include leaders like J. Oswald Sanders, Timothy Keller, Jerry Bridges, and many others.

Others wield influence by *power*. Power can be used for good or evil purposes. God sovereignly puts people in positions of power to be His instruments for good in society. Such was the case with William

Wilberforce, who was instrumental in the fight against slavery in England during the 1800s. Today, there are many political, government, and industry officials who use their influence for God. On the other hand, some use their power for selfish ends or even for evil goals.

Some people have influence because of their *wealth*. Wealth, of course, is a relative term. Any amount of money above what's needed to live comfortably can be considered wealth. Some analysts of our world believe wealth is the driving force behind all world power. Certainly, it's a major driving force. Possessing even moderate wealth exerts a profound effect on how an individual thinks and acts. It gives the illusion of influence of *person*, though it's actually the influence of *money*. And nothing is more fleeting than money.

When a person realizes the nature of wealth's influence, it can be used for great good—funding many benevolent and missionary activities in this needy world. It can also be used for evil.

People who have some measure of affluence need to realize that their personhood does not depend on their wealth. It's so easy to lose sight of that vital fact:

> The love of money is the first step toward all kinds of sin. Some people have even turned away from God because of their love for it, and as a result have pierced themselves with many sorrows.
>
> I TIMOTHY 6:10, TLB

Whether influence comes from person, performance, knowledge, power, or wealth, one thing is certain: It *will* fade. So often, the decrease in our influence is our own fault—our misuse of the instruments of influence we possess.

The Most Valuable Influence

The influence of person is the most valuable of all forms of influence. It's also extremely vulnerable. "As dead flies give perfume a bad smell, so a little folly outweighs wisdom and honor" (Ecclesiastes 10:1). "A good name is more desirable than great riches; to be esteemed is better than silver or gold" (Proverbs 22:1).

No one can remove your influence of person. Only you can. A little sin can ruin the greatest of reputations. The news around the Christian community attests to that fact. Except in rare cases, sin destroys influence and reputation for years, if not for a lifetime. Recovery of that influence, though not impossible, is exceedingly difficult. At times, a reputation is smeared by gossip and false accusations. The truth will triumph eventually for a person of character.

Our performance must eventually fade as age and diminished capacity reduce our effectiveness. Some of our top performances, like those of an aging athlete, will be memories of the past. In the secular world, the pattern is to cast off even the best of past performances. What matters in the world is "what can you do for me now?" If you've experienced this loss, you know the feelings of betrayal that come with these events.

Two Great Examples

As I think about influence, I think of J. Oswald Sanders, my friend and mentor. He was nearing his ninetieth birthday when he died—working on his last book. At age fifty, he'd left a prosperous career as an attorney in New Zealand to lead the China Inland Mission (now Overseas Missionary Fellowship)—quite a step down from that esteemed position in secular society.

After several years of leading the mission, he retired, only to take on the directorship of a Christian college—another step downward in the eyes of even the Christian world. Then he retired again and certainly deserved a rest. But rather than lying back and taking it easy, he accelerated, spending his last twenty years speaking around the world more than three hundred times per year. His influence grew rather than diminished. Though he never sought the limelight or tried to maintain his position, respect for him only grew.

Though Oswald never complained, I'm certain each of his changes in life came with some trauma and loss. Certainly, his personal losses were great. He was widowed twice. What was perceived as a loss of influence became a stairstep to greater influence.

And I think of another man who certainly seemed to have lost everything in terms of position, authority, and influence. That man was Chuck Colson. As someone ensconced in power alongside former president Nixon, Colson pulsated with power and influence. And he used them with skill and mastery.

Then, in the midst of the Watergate scandal, his world collapsed. When the storm subsided, he found himself in prison with no hope or future. He was washed up. Finished. Down for the count.

In *Born Again*, Colson tells the story of how he fell, came to understand that his only hope was in Jesus Christ, and experienced a personal conversion. He was a man with no influence, but now he had personal hope.

As he began to put the pieces of his life back together, Colson quietly developed a personal burden for prisoners and their families. Out of this burden, the ministry Prison Fellowship developed. Then came Faith and Justice Fellowship (a ministry to the judiciary) and finally Neighbors Who Care (a ministry to victims of crime).

Chuck Colson gained influence all over the nation as a respected and listened-to statesman. His shattered influence grew back to an influence of far greater and lasting magnitude. He was granted fifteen honorary doctorates. He was awarded the million-dollar Templeton Prize for Progress in Religion, which he donated entirely to Prison Fellowship.

Guarding Your Personal Influence

You may be saying, "But I'm no J. Oswald Sanders or Chuck Colson." No, but you can be—perhaps not in such a public way. I've known many men who lost their obvious position and influence (power) but kept going. They grew in character and depth. Some began to use their influence in different ways. They traded influence of power for influence of person. They adjusted their lives to their new circumstances, seeing the hand of God in their history and future.

One such person whom I knew and admired was Army Lieutenant General William K. Harrison. He was known as "the Christian general." General Douglas MacArthur appointed him as chief of the UN armistice delegation at the end of the Korean War because MacArthur trusted his integrity. General Harrison was a leader of the US Officers' Christian Fellowship, and he went on to write and speak broadly on Christian topics.

Knowledge is the most constant area of personal influence. Yet as time goes on, fewer and fewer young people will seek our counsel unless we keep renewing and refreshing our knowledge and wisdom. One older Navigator staff member told me sadly, "I know all the answers, but no one asks me questions anymore."

There's also the distinct possibility that our knowledge will become outdated. To keep influencing others, we must keep current. Knowledge of the Word never fades but must remain fresh and relevant. The quickest way for influence to be lost—short of sin—is to have an axe to grind or a prejudiced stand on issues. We can certainly develop our personal views on politics or culture, but we must be extremely careful how and when we express them.

Becoming old doesn't automatically make us wise. Younger people don't want to know how we did it in the old days. If we insist on presenting ancient history, they'll listen politely, but they won't inquire again.

Power and wealth are as fleeting as a puff of smoke. As soon as they wane, their influence disappears. In recent decades, I've seen a number of people undergo financial setbacks, bankruptcy, hard times, and lawsuits. In many cases, they experienced a loss of friends and a loss of respect, and they sensed a general distancing from the Christian community that once courted their favor. Yet if they grew in character, humility, and wisdom, they regained respect and influence.

Influence, properly used, is a gift from God. It's largely temporary, and it's especially vulnerable. Guard it by being enamored with your God, not your influence.

6

LOSS OF IDENTITY AND SIGNIFICANCE

ONCE PEOPLE HAVE PASSED from their "useful" times of life, are they no longer valid as persons? Do they just fade into the past like a dim memory, sitting in a nursing home, visited by tolerant relatives who would rather be somewhere else?

Everything inside us cries out, "No!"—because we know that such a decline is our destiny.

I've seen many men leave various positions of responsibility. Two of them left a lasting impression on me because of their contrast.

A close friend served under a dynamic four-star general in the army. The retirement parade for the general was everything you would expect for a departing hero. Parties and special dinners filled the weeks before his retirement. He left in a blaze of glory.

About two years later, the general lay in a hospital. He was dying. My friend, a chaplain, visited him. The chaplain rather innocently asked, "What was it like leaving such great responsibility and becoming an ordinary citizen?" Bitterness filled the general's voice as he replied, "We drove off the base in our recreational vehicle. Now I commanded nothing except the steering wheel on my RV—and my wife tells me where to turn!"

He died without purpose, having lost the only identity he valued.

In sharp contrast was Lieutenant General William K. Harrison, whom I mentioned in the last chapter. I remember talking to him about his career. When General Harrison retired, he stepped out into a new life with the vigor and optimism of a young man. His identity and self-image were not in being a general. He went on to serve on a seminary board and write a book on eschatology, and he was in demand as a speaker.

Both of these men reached the end of their lives having had a similar human identity but a radically different view of their real identity.

We know the day is coming when we'll be feeble and old. Who knows what we'll cling to then as our identity?

Then there's the question of what happens when we lose our identity in the prime of life. That loss affects each of us in a much different way.

Establishing Your Identity

Have you ever been in a social situation where no one knows you? Where no one pays any attention to you? You meet people, they give you a nod, and they move on. Your mind starts scheming for some way of establishing your identity. Usually, the first move is to let them know what your work is: I'm an engineer. I'm an attorney. I'm a builder. I'm a machinist. I'm an electrician. I'm a teacher. Our occupations provide us with a temporary identity. Then we begin to spell out which layer of the hierarchy we occupy—project engineer, vice president, partner, foreman. Then we feel our identity is more solid.

Other aspects of our lives begin to emerge and give more substance to our identity: our wealth, who we know, our accomplishments, the size of our home, our hobbies. Unconsciously, we build up an identity to which we cling all too tightly.

I'm not guiltless in this game. Many times I've found myself letting people know "who I really am." Sometimes it's for a legitimate connection with others, but all too often it's for my own ego.

Does this sound like a familiar pattern? Regardless of the stratum of society in which we live, what we do (hunting, fishing, golf) and what we have (money, boats, clothes) have a particular value in terms of our identity. And through the years, we build and protect this identity.

I've included the word *significance* in the title of this chapter. Identity and significance are closely related. Identity denotes what you do; significance represents the relative importance (to yourself or to others) of what you do. My significance is the value I place on my identity. We each want to be significant, to have value. Yet a delicate balance is required for our identity to serve us well.

Losing Your Identity

What happens when you lose that identity? And you will. You'll be demoted or fired, or you'll retire, or move, or lose that identity in some other way. Then the impact of the phrase "I am what I do" will begin to sink in.

What you do is not who you really are, of course. But in reality, that is how we think and feel.

For men, identity is so wrapped up in our work that we do not, or cannot, envision ourselves apart from it. That is why unemployment is so devastating to a man's ego. And it's why so many men die within two years of retiring.

When we lose our work identity, we're faced with the question *Who am I?* It's an appropriate question—one we should have faced years ago.

Linking our identity with our work is a two-edged sword. For those in higher positions, losing their jobs can be traumatic. And many who spend their lives (as my stepfather did) in more mundane jobs face the unspoken response, "Oh, you're just a _____"—fill in the blank with truck driver, factory worker, janitor, day laborer, store clerk, or any job that may not pay well or doesn't require recognized special skills. Each of those jobs should be performed with dignity. They're integral to our society and should be valued. But how many mothers have ever boasted, "My son digs ditches"? They want instead to say, "He's a doctor," or, "He's a corporate officer."

Many men cringe at their identity in the lower rungs of employment, wishing that people would give them credit for their intelligence, integrity, or family life. Minorities in our country feel this all too strongly, being placed in certain boxes of society. They're frequently judged by their skin color or ethnic origins, not their abilities. We must go beyond race and culture to give every person the opportunity to grow into an identity based on ability and performance.

Moving beyond a Wrong View of Identity

As a person of reasonable spiritual maturity, I thought I'd moved beyond this wrong view of my personhood. I come from a simple, lower-income family. I was the first in my family to attend a university. I found much of my new identity related to my education and being an Air Force officer.

One day, I remarked to Mary, "You know, there are some titles that stay with you for a lifetime, and I have two of them: PhD and general." I began the statement as a praise to God, but even in saying it, I revealed my own focus on identity. I'm as afflicted with the problem as any other man. And I don't like the thought that I haven't progressed further. Even as I write this, I see my need to grow in my view of myself.

It's hard to describe to people what The Navigators do, and it's especially difficult to describe it to nonbelievers. When I'm asked what I do, I often reply by saying what I used to do—I served on the faculty of the US Air Force Academy, or I worked in the space program. The identity struggle is always present. Some of the struggle relates to pride. Some of it is because of our humanity.

Sometimes our work identity can be used for good to open doors of communication. In the Bible, some people are referred to by what they do: Elijah the prophet, David the king, Paul the apostle, Peter the fisherman, Matthew the tax collector. Centuries ago in Europe, many names were connected to the work a person did.

Identifying ourselves with our work is not intrinsically wrong, but making that our only identity is troublesome. We're created in the image of God—*imago dei*. God created each one of us with a unique set of gifts and skills for the good of humanity. But we must remember that we're far more than what we do. All of us will eventually lose our work-related identities. We'll become a "used-to-be." The shock will come when we realize how much this identity meant to us. We'll feel a deep sense of loss. Many men will suffer depression. Many will die early due to the void of their work identity.

The more our personhood is wrapped up in our external identity, the more the loss of it will impact us.

The True Source of Identity

God clearly teaches the real source of identity in the Bible. Our identity is in Christ. We are sons and daughters of God, believers in Christ. God also gave us valid identities that distinguish us for a lifetime—human being, friend, neighbor, servant, father, husband. These identities can be wounded or broken, but they're legitimate, and we can build upon them.

Paul was a man of great accomplishments, but he counted them worthless compared to his identity in Christ. He reflected:

> Though I myself have reasons for such confidence.
>
> If someone else thinks they have reasons to put confidence in the flesh, I have more: circumcised on the eighth day, of the people of Israel, of the tribe of Benjamin, a Hebrew of Hebrews; in regard to the law, a Pharisee; as for zeal, persecuting the church; as for righteousness based on the law, faultless.
>
> But whatever were gains to me I now consider loss for the sake of Christ. What is more, I consider everything a loss because of the surpassing worth of knowing Christ Jesus my Lord, for whose sake I have lost all things. I consider them garbage, that I may gain Christ and be found in him, not having a righteousness of my own that comes from the law, but that which is through faith in Christ—the righteousness that comes from God on the basis of faith.
>
> PHILIPPIANS 3:4-9

This is a good theory, good teaching—but difficult to apply if it hasn't been a part of our foundation before the loss comes.

When my son was murdered, it was the spiritual roots that had grown deep earlier in my life that allowed me to draw upon the strength and comfort of God. My theology was tested, but my belief in the goodness and sovereignty of God ultimately deepened. Even more significant was the change in my identity as a man. Suddenly work and accomplishments meant almost nothing. Those things that previously fed my ego disappeared. My identity as a father, husband, friend, and frail human being emerged and deepened. My identity as a child of God took on new meaning, as did life itself.

Shifting from an identity based on human accomplishments to one based on our status as a child of God is a lifelong process. Any other identity will fail. Let's begin growing an identity that will last a lifetime.

LOSS OF CONFIDENCE

PERSONAL CONFIDENCE IS A MYSTERY. Some people have it; some don't. Confidence is self-reliance, the positive feeling that we can conquer the problems of life.

We want our children to develop confidence—to learn to walk, hit a baseball, recite a poem, build models, catch a football, play an instrument, give a speech.

We remember how we encouraged our babies to take their first steps. We watched them sit down abruptly rather than try taking steps.

When our children go to school, we want them to be confident and develop healthy self-esteem. I remember each of my children going through times of shyness, fear, and timidity. We worked with their fragile egos to encourage them, cheering at the smallest success, comforting them in each small failure. We may remember our own fear or loss of confidence when we tried out for a ball team or embarked on some new experience.

I clearly recall a confidence-building time in my senior year of high school. In the years that followed my separation from my grandfather,

I had lost my confidence. I became a believer in Christ before entering high school, and in my first semester as a high school freshman, I performed in an average fashion. I received one A, two Bs, and two Cs. Then I became a *committed* believer, making a definite commitment to the lordship of Christ. A light turned on within me. I'm not sure just how it happened, but when I became serious about walking with Jesus and publicly identifying with Him, my personal disciplines changed. I became a straight-A student, graduating with honors. What a confidence booster! I realized I could accomplish things, attain goals, and succeed.

Then an incident smashed my confidence.

I applied for a Navy ROTC scholarship at the University of Washington. I rode a Greyhound bus three hundred miles from Spokane to Seattle. I stayed overnight in the YMCA. The next morning, I appeared before a Navy captain for an interview. I was dressed in a sensible blue suit and a wash-and-wear (1950s-style) white shirt with a wrinkled collar. I looked like a country bumpkin. And I felt like one. I performed poorly in the interview.

When I said I liked music, the captain began to quiz me about classical composers—where they were born, what they wrote, where they lived. I didn't have a clue. I'd never studied classical music—I just liked to sing in the high school choir and play the accordion! I was embarrassed.

I wasn't awarded the scholarship. My confidence bubble burst. I went to the Air Force ROTC at the university as a default. Looking back, I find the incident somewhat humorous. But at the time, it was humiliating.

In that same time period, an incident happened that marked me permanently. In my high school American history class, I gave a verbal report on the Appomattox campaign in the American Civil War. When I finished, my teacher, Louis Livingston, said, "Now, that is the way a report should be given." What an incredible affirmation! Obviously—since I remember it after all these years—it made a great impact on me.

Self-Confidence: The Road to Success

As adult men, we know that self-confidence paves the way to success in many ways. As we mature, we learn and develop our gifts and skills, and we use them with confidence. Some men possess great confidence and have the talent to back it up. Others succeed with less talent but with strong confidence—sometimes bordering on bravado. Others of us fear that we'll be found lacking, so we mask our inner insecurities with an outer confidence.

By age thirty, most of us develop a reasonable confidence in ourselves and in our work. Then if some confidence-shaking event invades our lives, we feel we've been stripped bare. Whatever confidence we had begins to crumble.

My twenties and thirties were generally filled with confidence-building events. In my Air Force and Navigator careers, I experienced growing confidence and competence. But at age forty, the bottom fell out for me.

I'd been directing two geographical regions for The Navigators. I worked hard, too hard. There were numerous personnel problems and conflicts that needed attention. Every trip was emotion laden. Near the end of my first year of holding both jobs, I felt tired. But I realized the end was in sight, and I had some time planned for rest and recuperation.

Suddenly, I was asked to move to another part of the country to take yet another region. For me, that was the straw that broke the camel's back. I reacted. I became angry. Then I was embarrassed at my public reaction. Depression set in. Everyone could see it, or so I thought. I was physically and emotionally burned out.

I recovered fairly quickly. But my confidence was gone. I felt I had no place speaking out in leadership meetings. I didn't want any further responsibility. I felt I had failed. I imagined people talking about me: "Jerry has maxed out."

My prior work in The Navigators had gone well, but now my pride and ego were wounded. My limitations had been tested and broken. I lost confidence.

Through this experience I learned many valuable lessons. Over time, my confidence returned, but on a different and hopefully better foundation. It took me about a year to regain confidence and begin speaking out in meetings. It had been a time of brokenness. I'd begun to believe my own press clippings on capacity and ability. In retrospect, I was operating more in my own abilities, not in God's power.

The Sources of Self-Confidence

Where does confidence come from? Here are some of the sources:

Home Life

Personal background and family background form many of the roots of confidence. Affirming and encouraging children helps them develop healthy self-confidence and self-esteem. Children who face constant criticism grow up thinking they're incapable and incompetent. At the opposite extreme, children who are relentlessly pushed to the limits of their abilities grow up thinking they can never please their parents, thus wounding their developing confidence.

No one has a perfect upbringing. But parents who are confident will encourage confidence in their children. So much is absorbed in the context of the family. Positive attitudes, affirmation, appropriate discipline, stable relationships, and love cultivate the soil of confidence.

Neither affluence nor poverty determines confidence. We see people of confidence emerge from the most poverty-stricken homes as well as from wealthier environments. The key is what goes on inside the home.

Mary, my wife, comes from a stable and godly family. She always knew she was loved even though discipline and legalism were emphasized. I came from a divorced home but still had love. For both Mary and me, our parents had little in the way of worldly wealth or position, yet there was stability—our parents did the best they knew how to do in terms of encouragement. Could they have done better? Certainly. So could we with our children.

Regardless of your family background, you now have the responsibility to move forward in life. This is expressed by author Louis L'Amour:

Up to a point a man's life is shaped by environment, heredity, and movements and changes in the world about him; then there comes a time when it lies within his grasp to shape the clay of his life into the sort of thing he wishes to be. Only the weak blame parents, their race, their times, lack of good fortune, or the quirks of fate. Everyone has it within his power to say, this I am today, that I shall be tomorrow.[1]

This I am today; that I shall be tomorrow.

Again and again in our Navigator ministries with young people, I've seen transformation when young people come to faith in Jesus and begin (as I did) to experience the lordship of Christ. This counters some of the psychological emphasis placed on having a victim mentality. We cannot deny the sad incidents that have happened to us, but we must not forever be a victim.

Personality

Personality plays a significant role in our confidence. It's not a matter of being an extrovert or an introvert. Some people just naturally exude confidence. External confidence doesn't always indicate internal confidence, though. And even a naturally confident person can be broken by the events of life.

Norm and I met about twenty-five years ago. He was a new believer in Christ, full of energy and optimism. He was extremely successful in sales at a major computer company. As I watched him through the years, I observed him encounter many difficulties in life and business. Even when he was down, he was still positive and optimistic. This personality trait, combined with his growing faith, carried him through times when his confidence could have been destroyed. I often marveled at how he could be so positive. But that was simply the way God made him.

I think Norm did get discouraged. He wrestled internally with the "whys" of some of God's leading in his life. In fact, I suspect in some ways he was quite insecure, covering his insecurity with an external confidence. But Norm did show it to his close friends.

One other friend, Andy, had a similar personality. He always seemed to be up, though I knew he'd encountered some heavy issues in his life. But he was different from Norm. Andy never let it show, even to close friends. Later, Andy's life collapsed around him. He left his wife and family, destroying most of what had taken him a lifetime to build.

Natural Abilities and Performance

Competence is a tremendous confidence builder. It is simply the ability to perform a task well. Competence is a combination of natural gifts, training, and demonstrated experience. And just as there are good teachers and great teachers, good football players and great football players, good leaders and great leaders, so too there are varying degrees of competence.

We can always build competence in the areas in which we're gifted. Knowing our natural gifting is key to building competence. The apostle Paul instructs us to "think so as to have sound judgment" and "not to think more highly of [ourselves] than [we] ought to think" (Romans 12:3, NASB).

Franklyn was a dropout from college. He didn't even finish the first part of the first semester. He simply got bored and quit. One of his goals in life was to make money—lots of it. He soon got involved in a lucrative business that set him well on his way to financial success. In the process, he discovered he was really good at figuring out investments and making a profit.

He called me one day and asked if I knew anyone in a prestigious national brokerage firm. I asked why. He said he wanted to pursue that as a career. Firms like the one he wanted to join were hiring only people with Harvard MBAs or the equivalent. I reminded him he had no qualifications or education to make them even want to look at him.

But he persisted, talking his way into being hired. He finished number one in their training program—at age forty-two! He went on to do spectacularly well in the company. He was competent. It was clear that he was naturally gifted at understanding finance and handling money.

It's amazing to see the transformation of confidence that occurs when a man is in a job that matches his gifts and enhances his competence. When Franklyn matched his gifts and his job, his confidence soared.

However, even when you're competent, there will always be others who are more competent. Competence itself will not protect your job or your ego; it's only one factor. More is needed to put your confidence in the right place.

Educational Background

Education is a key component of confidence. Roland finished his stint in the Navy, having come to personal belief in Christ as a young sailor. He received help from The Navigators, so he joined our training program at Glen Eyrie. It was a program of work, study, and character building; some people joined our staff after completing it.

Roland had little education, came from a poor home, and was extremely awkward. He could hardly put together a grammatically complete sentence. Those who met him thought he had a mental disability, and they soon ushered him on to other things. He returned to his home state and enrolled in college. There he (and others) found that he in fact had a genius IQ.

Education began to awaken his curiosity, intellect, and incredible ability to think. Today, he's a highly respected academician, author, and apologist of Christianity. He went from defeat and discouragement to fulfillment and accomplishment through his dedication to both God and his education.

In a society where such a high value is placed on technical and academic education, we can never stop learning. The pace of change in every area of our society requires us to keep pursuing education and development. For someone who has "stalled out" or has lost confidence, returning to further study may be the key to rebuilding.

In The Navigators, I've seen many men whose lives were radically changed by their conversion experience. Even when they had no prior interest in schooling, after their conversion, they hungered to learn. As with Roland, education then transformed their lives and confidence.

The School of Experience

Experience contributes significantly to building or destroying confidence. This is especially true in the secular realm. The cumulative experiences of life either build us up or break us down. But we should never think that only successful experiences build confidence. Some of the most gifted and successful people in the world developed confidence through difficult and disastrous experiences. Through those experiences, they developed both character and confidence.

Allen decided to go to a small Bible school rather than a university. People wondered what good that would do him, since he didn't plan to go into a full-time ministry position. He got a job with an airline, slowly working his way up in marketing and management. Most of his contemporaries had education far beyond his.

When Allen took an early retirement, it was just a matter of months before the company asked if he would come back to tackle a difficult management task in another country. They wanted him specifically because of his experience, his character, and his demonstrated performance.

His past experiences weren't always easy, since he'd determined to live by God's rules without compromise. He hadn't cut corners or succumbed to pressures to promote himself or act unethically. When the need arose for someone who was experienced and also uncompromising in his standards, he was clearly the man.

Overcoming Confidence Shakers

Many events can cause us to lose our confidence. A few events can destroy it. Most confidence breakers relate to some failure or perceived failure in life and work. A poor performance review, the loss of a position or job, a failed marriage, a public embarrassment, burnout, an emotional breakdown, illness, or bankruptcy can trigger a deterioration of confidence. The crisis can happen suddenly, or it may develop over a long period of time. Repeated failures can also lead to diminished confidence.

Whatever the trigger, the root cause of the loss is a misplaced confidence. The only place we can safely put our confidence is in God. The Bible talks about depending on either the flesh or the Spirit. When the Bible speaks of the "flesh," it's referring to our baser human drives—often the gratification of sin.

When we depend solely on education, family background, personality, experience, or competence for our confidence, we're essentially depending on the flesh. Even though all of these are from God (1 Corinthians 4:7), when we depend on them alone, we're depending on ourselves, not God. "The mind set on the flesh is hostile toward God . . . those who are in the flesh cannot please God" (Romans 8:7-8, NASB).

If we focus on our achievements and abilities, we'll face disappointment, for they'll eventually fade. They cannot last forever. We need to shift our focus from ourselves to God, from our attributes to God's attributes, from depending on our flesh to depending on God. Only He can give us true satisfaction and confidence.

We regain confidence by putting our confidence in God. Confidence in the flesh says, "Look what *I* have done," or "Look who *I* am." God will not tolerate that arrogance. He insists that we find our fulfillment in Him, not in the world of accomplishments. He wants to root our confidence in His love and His grace.

8

THE ANTIDOTE FOR LOSS

MY WIFE, MARY, discovered a lump in her breast. She'd experienced this before, so we approached the lumpectomy without much concern. The surgeon came out of the operating room saying that all looked fine and that he'd ordered a routine biopsy.

When the results came back, we heard the dreaded word. *Cancer!*

Suddenly, life took on a different perspective. Consultations, reading, and discussions ensued to determine what should be done to cure or remove the cancer. We needed the right antidote—the best procedure.

The treatment we chose eradicated the cancer to the best of our knowledge. Through the process, we grew spiritually as we contemplated possible outcomes and losses.

Other friends haven't been so fortunate. One friend has a cancer that the doctors simply don't know how to treat. Chemotherapy was problematic. Our friend chose a nutritional route of therapy.

In every case, the final outcome rests with God. The medicine and the antidote differ. Various cancers require specific cures, cures that are not speculative but divinely and carefully chosen.

Having delved into the many losses that can overtake us when we least expect them, we now turn to practical and biblical cures. Before we were born, God already knew us as men and as individuals. He knew the traumas that would intrude into our lives—and He provided a cure.

Saul's Loss, Paul's Gain

Saul, the renegade Pharisee who became an apostle of Christ, knew about loss. He had everything going for him in his work for the Jewish leadership. His family background was superb. He was born an upper-class Jew as well as a Roman citizen. Educated under the famed Gamaliel, he took his place in society as a Pharisee. He rapidly made a name for himself as a persecutor of people of "the Way"—believers in Jesus as the Christ. He excelled in tormenting them.

Suddenly, his bubble burst as he traveled to Damascus to persecute more Christians. The story is told in Acts 9:1-9. He was struck blind in a confrontation with Jesus, who said to him, "Saul, Saul, why do you persecute me?" (9:4).

Recognizing that this was not a human interruption, Saul asked, "Who are you, Lord?" (9:5).

"I am Jesus" was the answer (9:5). Impossible! Jesus was dead! Yet Jesus talked to him, demanding attention via Saul's blindness. Saul was ready to listen.

I can imagine Saul's fear. His confidence eroded. His background, education, identity, motivation, and influence no longer gave him purpose. They disappeared in the blinding light that surrounded him. He feared Jesus, and he feared his loss of identity.

Saul was a man of integrity who now faced a difficult choice. This Jesus was real. Saul had to choose between his known identity and Christ. The loss he felt did battle with the personal revelation of Jesus as the Truth.

Later, Saul—who was also known as Paul (Acts 13:9)—reflected on his loss. He recounted his roots and achievements as a means for confidence:

If anyone else has a mind to put confidence in the flesh, I far more: circumcised the eighth day, of the nation of Israel, of the tribe of Benjamin, a Hebrew of Hebrews; as to the Law, a Pharisee; as to zeal, a persecutor of the church; as to the righteousness which is in the Law, found blameless.

PHILIPPIANS 3:4-6, NASB

Paul then assessed his loss:

But whatever things were gain to me, those things I have counted as loss for the sake of Christ. More than that, I count all things to be loss in view of the surpassing value of knowing Christ Jesus my Lord, for whom I have suffered the loss of all things, and count them but rubbish so that I may gain Christ, and may be found in Him, not having a righteousness of my own derived from the Law, but that which is through faith in Christ, the righteousness which comes from God on the basis of faith, that I may know Him and the power of His resurrection and the fellowship of His sufferings, being conformed to His death.

PHILIPPIANS 3:7-10, NASB

Paul's understanding of his loss did not come immediately. He suffered for his newfound faith. He wrestled with the trade-off. He probably wondered about his own sanity—as did the governor Festus when he remarked to Paul, "Your great learning is driving you insane" (Acts 26:24).

Paul knew he couldn't turn back from his encounter with Jesus. His conversion was genuine. He outlined the process of dealing with his loss:

1. He acknowledged his human inheritance and achievements.

2. He recognized them for what they were—useless rubbish.

3. He did not deny their importance or their effect on his life. He remained grateful for them.

4. He saw his loss as the doorway to a new life in Christ.

5. His motivation was replaced with a motivation founded on knowing Christ and experiencing the power of that new life and relationship. This resulted in him sharing his faith with Jews and Gentiles.

When Theory Penetrates the Mind and the Heart

At this point you may say, "Great theory. Been there, done that. Now what?"

Stop. You probably have *not* "been there, done that." This is not kindergarten material. This is the graduate school of human experience where the fundamentals of life take root.

I clearly remember my graduate school experience studying astronautics. Up to that time, I could pass tests, learn by rote, and give the right answers in my field. One professor started his class with the most basic concepts (of energy and mass) and rebuilt the theory. Lights flashed in my mind for the first time. I finally understood the why of what I'd been using in my profession.

The same thing happens in the spiritual realm. Knowledge must be married to understanding *in experience.*

I observe two kinds of men. The first is a man who has a personal relationship with Christ. He knows he has eternal life. When he's a young believer, some of the biblical concepts are new. He needs to walk through them slowly, wrestling with ideas and considering their implications.

More mature believers (as I was when I experienced my personal losses) tend to skim over the concepts. *Don't!* This is a time for dissecting and rebuilding in spiritual graduate school. The truth needs to penetrate the mind and the heart.

The second kind of man is one who's still on the way to Christ. He's not certain that faith in Christ is the real answer to life. But he's open to the idea. He senses the frustrations of mediocre achievements. He has begun to feel their loss, their insignificance, and to look elsewhere for answers. He may have tried a number of substitutes to compensate for loss.

Both types of men need deep and fundamental inner changes. One needs to deepen his understanding of his faith. The other needs to embark on that journey.

Keys to Responding to Loss

In dealing with losses in my own life, I've learned one major lesson: *I cannot control my circumstances, but I can control my response.*

Coming to this realization puts a major building block in place so that we can rebuild after experiencing loss. The key to living victoriously with loss is how we respond over time.

Note these two phrases: *how we respond* and *over time.*

Most of us cannot control our immediate response to loss. It simply takes time to reflect on losses, to understand our feelings about them, and to reorder our thinking. How we respond grows out of a series of realizations, concepts, and truths.

The most fundamental biblical truth is that *God is sovereign in all the circumstances of my life.* This means that God is all-knowing and in complete control. This cannot be explained in human terms. It goes beyond our ability to comprehend. We interact with these truths by the choices we make. This truth is expressed in both the Old and New Testaments.

> See now that I myself am he!
> There is no god besides me.
> I put to death and I bring to life,
> I have wounded and I will heal,
> and no one can deliver out of my hand.

DEUTERONOMY 32:39

The LORD brings death and makes alive;
    he brings down to the grave and raises up.
The LORD sends poverty and wealth;
    he humbles and he exalts.
He raises the poor from the dust
    and lifts the needy from the ash heap;
he seats them with princes
    and has them inherit a throne of honor.
For the foundations of the earth are the LORD's;
    on them he has set the world.

1 SAMUEL 2:6-8

God, the blessed and only Ruler, the King of kings and Lord of lords, who alone is immortal and who lives in unapproachable light, whom no one has seen or can see. To him be honor and might forever. Amen.

1 TIMOTHY 6:15-16

This is heavy theology—hard words. It's easier to talk of the love of God or the love of Jesus. Yet, not only is God sovereign; fortunately, His sovereignty *is* expressed in complete love and compassion. He knows our humanity and our frailty.

Paul expresses this truth memorably: "I'm absolutely convinced that nothing . . . absolutely *nothing* can get between us and God's love because of the way that Jesus our Master has embraced us" (Romans 8:38-39, MSG).

The Antidote for Loss: Choosing to Grow

God is sovereign, and He never places us in circumstances without purpose and design. Our awareness of that leads to the foundational concept that *a time of loss can be a time of great personal and spiritual growth.* It's through difficult circumstances that we grow. In many sports environments, the saying "No pain, no gain" is often posted in full view of the athletes. Similarly, in the Christian life, little growth occurs without discipline and pain.

But how do we grow? How are we strengthened?

We grow in character. We grow in our inner person. We begin to develop those qualities of life that are most valuable: "love, joy, peace, patience, kindness, goodness, faithfulness, gentleness and self-control" (Galatians 5:22-23, TLB). The sad alternative is anger, bitterness, and resentment, which together lead to depression and deep loneliness. The middle ground between those two extremes is worse—a deadening of spirit, separation from God, a refusal to feel, and the death of your life purpose.

We grow in making choices. We choose. We choose our responses. At first it seems contrived or technical. Even the apostle Paul had to learn to respond properly: "I have learned to be content whatever the circumstances" (Philippians 4:11).

What do we choose?

1. We choose to believe that God is in control. But we must act on that belief.
2. We choose to believe that everything we have is from God.

My intellect, my background, my abilities, my opportunities, and my achievements all come from God: Did I make choices to act on these? Of course. Did others open doors for me? Yes.

> Is there anything they would discover in you that you could take credit for? Isn't everything you *have* and everything you *are* sheer gifts from God? So what's the point of all this comparing and competing? You already have all you need. You already have more access to God than you can handle.
>
> I CORINTHIANS 4:7-8, MSG

How about our personal effort? I chose to work hard within the realm of the gifts and abilities God gave me. That effort is a critical

factor. We cannot just sit back and expect God to act with no coopera-
tion on our part.

1. *We choose to acknowledge our frailty and humanity.* Learn to count
   every day as a gift from God. Live for what's really important in
   life. As I've mentioned, one of the greatest lessons that came to
   me as a result of my son's death was the realization that what I'd
   valued in an earthly sense was of little worth. Eternal values are
   paramount. Position, influence, and identity are as transient as a
   puff of breath on a frosty day—momentarily visible, then gone.

2. *We choose to examine our motives as related to our value system.*
   Are the things that give you motivation and confidence really
   worthwhile? Are you depending on your position, identity, and
   influence for your self-worth?

3. *We choose to rebuild our lives on a better foundation.* That foundation is expressed by Paul: "I want to know Christ" and "the
   power of his resurrection" (Philippians 3:10). A desire to please
   and serve God and to live for family and others, not ourselves,
   becomes our motivation.

We also grow through training. From how the Bible portrays losses,
we can learn to recognize them as opportunities for growth. They're not
punishments but training. As a master trainer or coach teaches us, so
God trains us.

This is a complex argument. Tragic events happen to us—abuse,
violence, injustice, unfair treatment. All of these reflect the evil in our
world. The theological discussion of evil is beyond the scope of this
book, but take note that throughout the Scriptures, God used evil for
His good purposes.

In Genesis, we see how Joseph, who was so terribly abused by his
brothers, was able to tell them, "You intended to harm me, but God
intended it for good to accomplish what is now being done, the saving
of many lives" (Genesis 50:20).[1]

God's Purpose in Loss

God disciplines His disciples in terms those of us who are fathers understand—the discipline (not punishment) of our children for their good:

Have you completely forgotten this word of encouragement that addresses you as a father addresses his son? It says,

"My son, do not make light of the Lord's discipline,
and do not lose heart when he rebukes you. . . ."

Endure hardship as discipline; God is treating you as his children. For what children are not disciplined by their father? If you are not disciplined—and everyone undergoes discipline—then you are not legitimate, not true sons and daughters at all. . . . No discipline seems pleasant at the time, but painful. Later on, however, it produces a harvest of righteousness and peace for those who have been trained by it.

HEBREWS 12:5-11

God's purpose is this "harvest of righteousness"—right living that pleases Him. Discipline produces a beautiful harvest of deep inner peace in our lives.

My friend and mentor J. Oswald Sanders endured and overcame much loss. Before he was fifty, he was afflicted with arthritis so badly that he could hardly get out of bed. In the prime of his midlife, it appeared that he would be permanently limited physically. But he kept moving. He kept working. As he entered his second and third careers (following his service as a lawyer, as general director of China Inland Mission and then as principal of a Bible college), he was totally freed from arthritis. He could have given up. He could have taken a nice retirement. Instead, he entered into what many would say were the most productive years of his life.

He wrote:

> The discipline is always preparatory to blessing and can bring
> nothing but blessing when rightly received. It is here that our
> responsibility lies. Food not digested is a bane, not a blessing.
> Disciplines not rightly received sour rather than sweeten the
> character. To querulously ask "Why?" when the chastening
> stroke falls is in effect to charge the all-wise and all-loving God
> with caprice. *He does not rend the heart merely to demonstrate His
> power and sovereignty but to prepare for greater fruitfulness.* He
> prunes every branch that does bear fruit to increase its yield.
> The discipline is purposeful. How do we react to God's plow?
> Does it soften, subdue, chasten us? Or does it harden and
> stiffen our resistance to His will? Does it sweeten or sour us?[2]

He continued by saying that God has three purposes in the discipline:
personal, to cultivate the soul; *relative,* to provide food (blessing) to
others; and *ultimate,* to prepare us for heaven.

Sanders then quoted Alexander Whyte:

> We cease to wonder so much at the care God takes of human
> character . . . and the cost He lays out upon it, when we think
> that it is the only work of His hands that shall last forever. . . .
> Riches, honor, possessions, pleasures of all kinds; death with
> one stroke of his desolate hand shall one day strip us bare to a
> winding sheet and a coffin of all the things we are so mad to
> possess.[3]

(Excellent discussions on this topic can be found in two books by Philip
Yancey: *Where Is God When It Hurts?* and *Disappointment with God.*)[4]

There's so much more to life. We must not allow temporal losses to
detour us from becoming the best we can be in Christ. That's the unseen
danger—that we fail to gain strength in our losses, the strength to
respond to loss with a learner's spirit and deeper growth in true character.

PART TWO

Sin's Dangers for Men

9

THE REALITY OF SIN

SIN. Such a cold word. Such a hard word. If only we could just call sin *a mistake, a lapse of judgment,* or *a failure.*

We fear sin—yet we're drawn irresistibly to it in so many areas of life. Consider these heroes of faith:

- Noah was a man who sinned in his old age.
- Samson was a man who sinned in his youth.
- David was a man who sinned in his success.
- Saul was a man who sinned in his pride.

Man after man in the Bible stumbled along the way. Few finished well. Men like Moses, Noah, and David were scattered among the wreckage of men who started well but succumbed to sin. Sin overtook them and destroyed years of credibility.

Of all dangers, sin is the most potent. It destroys, maims, and cripples.

The first brothers in human history, Cain and Abel, felt the disastrous impact of sin in their lives and family. Each came to God with an offering. Cain brought a grain offering. Abel brought an animal from his flock. God accepted Abel's offering but not Cain's. The Bible doesn't record the reason for God's displeasure with Cain's offering. Cain's problem may have been attitude or sincerity. Cain's response reflected what resided in his heart. "So Cain became very angry and his countenance fell" (Genesis 4:5, NASB). Anger gripped him. Discouragement infected his spirit.

God was not angry with Cain but was trying to help him deal with the problems of his heart.

> Then the Lord said to Cain, "Why are you angry? And why has your countenance fallen? If you do well, will not your countenance be lifted up? And if you do not do well, *sin is crouching at the door; and its desire is for you, but you must master it.*"
>
> GENESIS 4:6-7, NASB, EMPHASIS ADDED

What a terrifying word picture! In Kenya, I observed a lioness stalking her prey. She stopped behind a bush and bent her powerful legs. Her body tensed to spring on her target and destroy it. Peter uses a similar word picture: "Your adversary, the devil, prowls around like a roaring lion, seeking someone to devour" (1 Peter 5:8, NASB).

As you've probably recognized, many dangers addressed in this book are like that. Unexpected. Surprises. Without warning. Even though we're aware of the possibility of the danger, we cannot imagine it will happen to us. No matter how old we are or how mature we are spiritually, we're always vulnerable.

Before identifying specific sins, it's important to understand more about the biblical view of sin, including its nature and power. Otherwise, we might simply review a list of sins that plague most of us in an attempt to frighten ourselves into not committing them.

The Nature of Sin

It's helpful to know the reasons behind any admonition to do or not do something. As a young believer, I was given prohibitions to avoid alcohol, dancing, movies, smoking, and other activities. I was aware that some Christians thought these activities were sinful. I didn't know the biblical basis for their reasoning. The effect was to engender confusion regarding the seriousness of sin. I was given some rules but no biblical instruction on specific acts and the theological context of sin.

Most of us have the desire expressed in these scriptural words: "Direct my footsteps according to your word; let no sin rule over me" (Psalm 119:133). No man wants to have sin ruling or dominating him. We want to have a clear conscience and a pure heart.

As we work toward the goal of a life free from the bondage of sin, we need to more fully understand the nature of sin.

Two issues seem to plague every thinking believer in Christ:

1. A lack of a lifetime commitment to Christ's lordship
2. Sins that seem to persist in our lives despite their being discouraged

Overcoming Sin

The key to overcoming these problems resides in the crucified life, as summarized and reinforced by Paul in these words:

> I have been crucified with Christ and I no longer live, but Christ lives in me. The life I now live in the body, I live by faith in the Son of God, who loved me and gave himself for me. I do not set aside the grace of God, for if righteousness could be gained through the law, Christ died for nothing!
>
> GALATIANS 2:20-21

For we know that our old self was crucified with him so that
the body ruled by sin might be done away with, that we should
no longer be slaves to sin—because anyone who has died has
been set free from sin.

ROMANS 6:6-7

We live with the dilemma of sin. Clearly, we're no longer under the
law, attempting to please God by our good deeds. We're under grace.
Our salvation comes by grace through faith. We don't earn it. We're
saved from the penalty of sin. The dilemma is: Why do we persist in
certain sins?

Why Do We Keep Sinning?

A thorough study of Romans 5 and 6 helps answer this question. In
Romans 4, Paul recounts the experience of Abraham—particularly
how Abraham received his salvation by grace, not by works. When
Abraham trusted God to fulfill His promise to provide a son as an
heir, "it was credited to him as righteousness" (Romans 4:22; see also
Genesis 15).

The words "it was credited to him" were written not for him
alone, but also for us, to whom God will credit righteousness—
for us who believe in him who raised Jesus our Lord from the
dead. He was delivered over to death for our sins and was raised
to life for our justification.

Therefore, since we have been justified through faith, we
have peace with God through our Lord Jesus Christ, through
whom we have gained access by faith into this grace in which
we now stand.

ROMANS 4:23–5:2

We need to look at this passage as an attorney would look at a con-
tract, examining every word and phrase. Here are the key concepts:

- We receive God's unearned favor (grace) when we place our faith (believe) in Christ and His death for our sins and His victory over death in resurrection.

- We're then justified—righteousness is credited to our account. This is a legal term meaning that the debt or charges against us are totally erased and forgiven.

- We have peace with God—there is no remaining debt to be paid.

- Our residence (where we stand) is "in Christ." We're totally under the roof of His protection.

We have no further penalty to pay for our sin. It has been fully paid by Christ in His death on the cross. However, even though we're now dead to sin in terms of its future power over us, we're still susceptible to its presence and influence. And Satan still has power to tempt and influence us.

The Power of Sin Shattered

At this point, we need to contrast *sin* (singular) and *sins* (plural):

> Therefore, just as sin [singular] entered the world through one man [Adam], and death through sin [singular], and in this way death came to all people, because all sinned—
> To be sure, sin was in the world [through Adam's sin] before the law was given. . . .
> Consequently, just as one trespass resulted in condemnation for all people, so also one righteous act resulted in justification and life for all people.
> ROMANS 5:12-13, 18

The external power of sin and the penalty of sin have been forever shattered. The old self died with Christ. We are now a new creation (2 Corinthians 5:17). The result of this death is twofold:

1. Our new life here and our resurrection to eternal life are assured. We're free from the penalty of sin. *Sin shall not be our master.* Satan's power is broken.

2. *We are no longer slaves to sin.* Sin no longer has legal power over us. But we still need to choose to be free in our present actions.

Even though we're free, we can choose to live as slaves. Sin has lost its power over us, but sins and sinning still plague our human lives. Our old selves died with Christ, but our fleshly human nature still lives. Before we came to faith in Christ, we did not have the divine power to resist sin. It's true that some nonbelievers live outwardly upright lives, resisting many sins by their own choice, but their power is limited and not from the Holy Spirit.

For believers in Jesus Christ, His power living in us now gives us every resource we need to resist a life of sin. Therefore, Paul says: "Count yourselves dead to sin" (Romans 6:11). That means that we're now to act on the reality that the old self is dead.

Freedom from Sin

Picture yourself in a prison cell on death row, having been sentenced to death. A judge suddenly pardons you and orders your freedom. The cell doors open. But you decide to stay in prison. You are free, and you will not be executed. But you don't leave, and you don't exercise your freedom. This is a picture of a believer who is free but chooses to continue letting sins invade his life. He fails to accept his freedom.

Paul's words in Romans 6:11 are paraphrased by *The Living Bible* in this way: "So look upon your old sin nature as dead and unresponsive to sin, and instead be alive to God, alert to him, through Jesus Christ our Lord."

Act on the fact! The phrase "live in reality" reflects this truth. We all know people who fail to accept the reality about their financial, moral, or ethical circumstances. Many people live in a world of captivity to sin. The captivity is so real that we easily believe there's no escape. This leads to fear and incapacity.

We need to act on truth—the truth that we have died to sin in Christ. That's our position. We need to live now in accordance with our position as sons of God, turning away from our sinful behavior.

We're like the multimillion-dollar lottery winner who has the choice of continuing to live as a pauper or using the wealth to bring himself out of poverty.

We still need to fully answer the question, "Why do I keep on sinning if I've died to sin?" Sin no longer possesses unbreakable power over us, but it remains a powerful force. I still have the propensity and the ability to sin. If I did not, why would the following words from the apostle John be such a key passage for believers?

> If we confess our sins, he is faithful and just and will forgive us our sins and purify us from all unrighteousness. If we claim we have not sinned, we make him out to be a liar and his word is not in us.
>
> 1 JOHN 1:9-10

In these verses, confession is not for salvation but rather for cleansing the conscience before God. This enhances our fellowship and walk with God. We still live with the human consequences of our sins.

We see the notion of freedom from sin alongside the potential for ongoing sin in these words from Paul: "You have been set free from sin . . . and the result is eternal life" (Romans 6:22). Because of this reality of freedom, Paul tells us, "Do not let sin reign in your mortal body so that you obey its evil desires" (Romans 6:12). We now have a choice. Before salvation, we had no choice—we followed sin blindly. As believers, we possess the power of the Holy Spirit to make godly choices in spite of the flesh and our sinful nature, which will plague us until physical death.

We're freed from the penalty of sin, but we are not free from sin's influence. Our choices are these:

- Serve sin—in the flesh.
- Serve righteousness—in the Spirit.

Later I'll discuss the practical application of these truths in living a Spirit-led life. First, let's consider four of the unexpected dangers of sin, which can so easily sneak up on men, like a lion stalking its prey.

WHEN SEXUAL TEMPTATION BECOMES SIN

ONE OF MY FRIENDS, CLIFF, had been moving toward Christ for a number of years. Several times he was almost ready to commit his life to Christ. He told me, "I started going to church. Then the pastor ran off with the organist. It seemed that every time I reached a place where I trusted a Christian, they did some dumb thing like that, so I backed off."

We all know more stories like that than we care to count. Yet even as we observe others fall, we think we're immune.

We are not immune. Disaster can strike any of us. We live with the danger described in this verse: "The prudent see danger and take refuge, but the simple keep going and pay the penalty" (Proverbs 22:3). We see the danger, yet we keep going, and it ends up hurting us greatly.

Perhaps you have a past marked by sexual sin, or perhaps sexual sin marks your present life. You may be trapped by an addiction to illicit sex, pornography, or some other sexual sin. If so, don't despair or skip this chapter just because you've tried many times to overcome your sin and failed.

There *is* a way out. God forgives completely. There's no sin He doesn't forgive. But persistent or habitual sin will not loosen its hold easily. That's what these next chapters are all about.

What Is Temptation?

We would all agree that certain acts of sexual immorality are sinful. But what about sexual activities of mind and body that we think fall short of immorality? What do we do with temptations in those areas?

We're all tempted. All men struggle with sexual temptation. We're drawn like magnets to "the lust of the flesh and the lust of the eyes" (1 John 2:16, NASB).

What is temptation? Synonyms for *tempt* include *allure, attract, entice, seduce,* and *tantalize.* Synonyms for *tempted* include *enchanted, entranced, bewitched, hypnotized, spellbound, charmed, mesmerized, enraptured,* and *captivated.* Each of these words generates an emotional picture. Temptation relates to sin. Men are allured by it. We're attracted to it, enticed by it, seduced by its seeming pleasure, tantalized by the fantasy of what it would be like. We experience sexual temptation daily. We look at women and encounter sexual thoughts. Jokes in the workplace among men often have sexual overtones. Almost unbidden, our minds conjure up sexual thoughts. It's our plague, our persistent sickness.

In reflecting on sexual issues, we must not forget that sex is God's idea. It was made as the ultimate fulfillment of the union between a man and a woman in marriage for procreation and pleasure. When we take it outside the marital bond it becomes sin, though it can be misused in marriage also.

I also acknowledge that many people (if not most) in today's culture consider sex outside marriage as normal and healthy. Even among some Christians, it's not the taboo it once was. But that's a reflection of culture, not of Scripture.

The Ultimate Risk for Men

If I were writing this book to women, would I include sexual temptation as a major danger? Yes, but not in the same way. Women are certainly tempted sexually. But the drive and the motive are different. According to Robert Hicks in *The Masculine Journey*, sex is not the hourly frontal lobe preoccupation for most women that it is for most men. Women generally want intimacy, communication, and relationship in the context of security and family more than physical sex.[1]

Men seem to be easily driven to extreme behavior. This drive is focused primarily on sex, power, and money—probably in that order.

The power they seek is over people, circumstances, their own lives, and their wives and children.

The drive for money is a persistent force throughout a man's life. He rarely has enough. Whether he is wealthy or not, a man pushes to make money. Sometimes it is simply to provide for his family. Often it is to provide a sense of worth and security.

Both money and power obsessions can lead to sinful behaviors. But sex and sexual temptation fall into a class all their own.

When men choose to violate the scriptural intention for sex (that is, sex in the context of marriage), it becomes the ultimate risk.

As Robert Hicks comments, "Many men get stuck in Phallic City, though it is a normal part of developing manhood. It begins in adolescence and continues throughout the life span."[2]

Sexual Temptation Starts in the Mind

Sexual temptation is *not* primarily physical. It begins in the mind. In another book I wrote, I noted the following:

> Sexual sin never begins by accident. People do not suddenly fall into an illicit sexual act simply by having an opportunity confront them. There is always some specific preparation. This preparation we call "pre-sexual" experience. Pre-sexual experiences are those experiences of mind and action which excite, train, or develop our sexual drives.[3]

Sexual temptation is an issue of the mind. The mind can act only on what it has confronted through what we have seen, read, or heard. Our other senses—touch, taste, and smell—may be engaged as well. Therefore, to guard against sexual temptation, we must be careful about what we look at, read, listen to, or touch. Images are planted that cause lust to take hold. Even when we don't act immorally, we can be polluted by a mental and emotional fixation on sex. Movies, television, and video mediums have become more and more graphic, and we have become more tolerant of it. At least I know I have, just observing how my own acceptance of what I view has changed over the years.

The Power of Porn

Pornography in its many forms can so easily get a foothold in our lives. In *The Masculine Journey*, Robert Hicks writes:

> The real power of pornography is that it provides men with the ultimate fantasy fulfillment without the risk of emotional rejection that often accompanies relationship with "real" women. In normal sexual relations, our fragile male egos are on the line, and often the slightest rejection of our advances can drive us quickly into seclusion, brooding, and hurt. Pornography solves the problem. There exists a seemingly unceasing supply of super attractive, inviting women, always available, always willing—and who give the impression that each reader [viewer] is very special.

Hicks then makes this profound conclusion: "Pornographic literature plays with our minds at the deepest levels."[4]

Although we are focusing on the harm pornography does to men, we must never forget that it also degrades women. Women are trapped in the sex trade worldwide. It's a travesty beyond belief. Sex trafficking and pornography have mushroomed into multitrillion-dollar industries.

Pornography doesn't just hinder us; it destroys us. Our walk with God is hindered by images that will not leave us. The danger is that it starts with minor indiscretions, seemingly harmless. Then it tantalizes us until we're caught in its web. You may know firsthand the despair, guilt, and helplessness that come with this practice. We hide from God. We become ashamed of our lust, making a tender relationship with God a sham.

For men, pornography is most often linked to masturbation. In spite of the blessing the secular world gives to this practice, declaring it normal, we know that it connects to poisonous sexual images in our minds. Masturbation feeds on visual images to excite us. (An excellent book to help men struggling with masturbation is *The War Within: Gaining Victory in the Battle for Sexual Purity* by Robert Daniels.[5] Another excellent study is Lonnie Berger's *Every Man a Warrior*, a comprehensive set of men's Bible studies that examines these sexual issues in depth, as well as many other topics.[6])

Caught in the Grip

A few months after our son was murdered, Mary and I went on a ministry trip to Thailand. Close friends asked us to go with them for three days to a resort on the coast. It was an incredibly beautiful setting. Cottages were perched on a lush hillside. A small sandy beach was nestled in the rocks about one hundred feet below the cottages.

Late the first afternoon, I decided to go for a short swim. The beach area was deserted. I swam about one hundred feet out, enjoying the tropical waters. I turned to swim to the shore and found I was caught in an outflowing current and could not make any headway toward land. I imagined being swept out to sea. I knew enough to swim parallel to the beach toward the rocky curve of the inlet. But the sea bottom was coral. I stumbled out after cutting my legs and hands on the coral. Thankfully, I made it.

At dinner that night, I sheepishly told our friends what had happened.

A strange smile crossed my friend's face. He said, "The same thing happened to me about half an hour before it happened to you." He had to call out, and a lifeguard came to help him.

That experience mirrors what sexual temptation does to us. It looks so pleasant and enjoyable. Then we get caught in its grip. We struggle to get out, but we're ensnared and bruised in the process. We often don't see the real danger until it's too late.

I didn't swim in that cove again!

Pornography is like that. It catches us and drives us deeper and deeper.

The statistics on porn use by men are frightening and overwhelming. Excellent research on the topic is being conducted by Barna Group and Josh McDowell Ministries (www.barna.com and www.josh.org). The following summarized statistics come from their research.

1. Ninety percent of boys are exposed to pornography by age eighteen.
2. Sixty-eight percent of adult men watch pornography at least once a week.
3. There are approximately forty-two mission porn websites, totaling about 370 million pages of porn.
4. Fifty-six percent of American divorces involve one party having an "obsessive interest" in pornographic websites.
5. Fifty-five percent of married men view pornography.

Pornography is a pandemic of monumental proportions. Yet statistics will not frighten us enough to solve the problem. The availability is unstoppable. The solution rests with each man and his family and accountability circle.

The guilt and shame we feel as a result of viewing pornography is enormous. Unfortunately, porn is increasingly seen as acceptable among young people, like casual sex. As men, we must not only address this issue but also make it a topic of emphasis in our churches and with our close friends. This destructive issue is worthy of a major battle plan.

The Sources of Sexual Temptation

What causes sexual temptation?

It comes from Satan and our flesh (our natural sinful inclination). What James says about temptation seems particularly true about sexual temptation (though we must remember that temptation is far broader than just sexual temptation; it embraces money, power, ego, and more):

> When tempted, no one should say, "God is tempting me." For God cannot be tempted by evil, nor does he tempt anyone; but each person is tempted when they are dragged away by their own evil desire and enticed.
>
> JAMES 1:13-14

Remember that for the believer, the sinful nature died with Christ. It no longer has irresistible power over us. We *can* choose—and therefore *must* choose. Temptation is placed before us, but by the Holy Spirit, we possess the power to withstand it.

That's the teaching we see in the New Testament, as in these words of Paul:

> No temptation has overtaken you except what is common to mankind. And God is faithful; he will not let you be tempted beyond what you can bear. But when you are tempted, he will also provide a way out so that you can endure it.
>
> I CORINTHIANS 10:13

Temptation is the common experience of all men, but God always provides a way out. However, note the verse just before this one: "If you think you are standing firm, be careful that you don't fall!" (1 Corinthians 10:12). We are all vulnerable. We all must be on the alert.

Principles for Dealing with Sexuality

Several years ago, I took a number of our Navigator leadership couples on a four-day whitewater rafting trip down the Green River in Utah. It's an amazingly beautiful wilderness area in the Dinosaur National Monument. Each night we slept in tents along the river. Just before leaving on that trip, I found out that a friend, a Christian leader known to many of us, had publicly confessed to sexual sin. I was greatly troubled. In spite of the pristine beauty of the place, the clear air, and the relaxing atmosphere, I couldn't sleep. In the middle of the night, I took my flashlight and walked out from the camp, sat down, and wrote the following letter to the men on my newsletter list:

Dear friends,

As I lay awake for about three hours one night in June, I felt personally burdened to share some thoughts with the men on our newsletter list. This is neither a newsletter nor a prayer letter, but rather a simple expression of some ideas that I hope will stimulate your thinking.

In view of some recent events, I think we need to honestly discuss the issue of sexual purity. I am addressing men since I am a man and can only speak from that perspective. But as women read this letter, it will help them understand the issues from a man's viewpoint.

Sexual purity is a direct command of Scripture. "For this is the will of God, your sanctification; that is, that you abstain from sexual immorality" (1 Thessalonians 4:3, NASB). There are no excuses. Repentance, yes. Forgiveness, yes. Excuses, no. And for some reason, the results of sexual sin, though sins are not graded by God, seem much more far reaching.

Here are some principles . . . thoughts . . . observations:

1. Sexual sin is always generated in the mind before it is acted out in the body. Thus, to guard one's thoughts is absolutely indispensable.

2. *A struggling marriage is never an excuse for sexual sin.*

3. *A widowed person, divorced person, or sexually experienced man will likely have more temptation, mainly due to knowledge.*

4. *In cases I have seen, some common threads emerge and seem characteristic of men who have fallen into sexual impurity:*
   - *The macho image and a sense of dominance*
   - *A perceived failure in one's job or a blow to one's ego or pride*
   - *A feeling of being "above the rules"*
   - *Going easy on oneself . . . in many areas, like diet or exercise*
   - *Carelessly allowing oneself to be in places or situations that boost temptation*
   - *A roving and undisciplined eye*

5. *Accountability is a major key to prevention, though not the only answer.*

6. *Even with accountability, one who wants to sin sexually will find a way to lie and deceive others, and himself, to avoid the truth. Thus, we must uphold one another with prayer.*

7. *Regardless of spiritual maturity or chronological age or the best of marriages, everyone is vulnerable to sexual sin.*

How can I have accountability? I suggest having someone ask you direct questions at least periodically—perhaps monthly. Here are some possibilities:

1. *Are you involved sexually with anyone other than your wife?*

2. *Are you using pornography?*

3. *Are you masturbating? (This is certainly a controversial issue. I suggest you examine the chapter on sexual morality in my book* Honesty, Morality, and Conscience. *Many believe that masturbation is not a serious issue. I tend to view it differently.)*

4. Are you watching R- or X-rated movies or videos?
5. Are you indulging in sexual fantasies about other women?

But after all of this, we might ask, "What are some of the best preventive measures against sexual sin?" Here are some suggestions:

1. Daily time with God in His Word and a commitment to spiritual growth
2. A commitment to the battle for winning the lost
3. A committed accountability relationship with one or two other men
4. A deepening marriage relationship with your wife
5. A constant guard in your thought life and actions
6. Determined and continually renewed commitment that you will not enter into sexual sin
7. Defensive prayer

Chuck Swindoll, in his book Growing Strong in the Seasons of Life, *made some insightful comments regarding Solomon:*

> Deterioration is never sudden. *No garden "suddenly" overgrows with thorns. No church "suddenly" splits. No building "suddenly" crumbles. No marriage "suddenly" breaks down. No nation "suddenly" becomes a mediocre power. No person "suddenly" becomes base. Slowly, almost imperceptibly, certain things are accepted that once were rejected. Things once considered hurtful are now secretly tolerated. At the outset it appears harmless, perhaps even exciting, but the wedge it brings leaves a gap that grows wider as moral erosion joins hands with spiritual decay. The gap becomes a canyon. That "way which seems right" becomes, in fact, "the way of death." Solomon wrote that. He ought to know.*

Take heed, you who stand: take heed lest you fall! Be careful about changing your standard so that it corresponds with your desires. Be very cautious about becoming inflated with thoughts of your own importance. Be alert to the pitfalls of prosperity and success. Should God grant riches, fame, and success, don't run scared or feel guilty. Just stay balanced. Remember Solomon, who deteriorated from a humble man of wisdom to a vain fool in a rather brief span of time.[7]

Yours in Christ,
Dr. Jerry White

In the intervening years, thousands of copies of that letter have been reproduced and read in men's groups. Why? Because every man recognizes his vulnerability and sincerely wants to prevent a fall.

(Please feel free to reproduce and distribute this letter. And please reference this book as its source.)

The Motivation behind the Principles

What is our motivation to avoid sexual sin? You'll likely say, "Fear!" Fear is a strong motivator. "Fear God and keep his commandments" (Ecclesiastes 12:13). "It is a fearful thing to fall into the hands of the living God" (Hebrews 10:31, KJV).

But fear is not enough. Fear works well only when we're facing an immediate consequence, such as having our sin suddenly exposed or discovered: "When the sentence for a crime is not quickly carried out, people's hearts are filled with schemes to do wrong" (Ecclesiastes 8:11).

Often, we practice sexual activities that we may view as falling short of immorality, and we observe that life seems to go on. I'm speaking of viewing pornography, indulging in mental fantasies, engaging in sexual activities short of intercourse while dating, etc. We think, *Where's God?*

When will I be found out? When will the lightning strike? Like tentatively stepping into cold water on a beach, we soon get used to it, and we venture deeper toward danger as we give in to sexual temptation. Fear is a temporary stopgap measure, a warning.

Our primary motivation for avoiding sexual sin is that we are the image of Christ and we don't want to stain that image. We want to live a pure and holy life. We want to be slaves of righteousness, not slaves to sin (Romans 6:18). Sexual sin can be very selfish. We sin against our wives and against women in general when we embark on our own sexual gratification. It's not just between us and God; it spills over into many relationships.

In his classic discussion of sexual immorality, Paul clarifies the motivation for purity:

> Do you not know that your bodies are temples of the Holy Spirit, who is in you, whom you have received from God? You are not your own; you were bought at a price. Therefore honor God with your bodies.
>
> I CORINTHIANS 6:19-20

In the Old Testament, Israel often abandoned God. He likened His disobedient people to women prostituting themselves sexually to other gods. Much of the worship of false gods included immorality with temple prostitutes. God *always* held them accountable.

Most men I know truly want to please God and to live a pure and holy life. They hate the habits of mind and body that enslave them. They want release. That release is available. It comes through confession, repentance, forgiveness, and spiritual renewal.

Guidelines for Handling Temptations

The book of Proverbs is specific and graphic in its warning against sexual temptation and sexual immorality:

I was looking out the window of my house one day and saw
a simpleminded lad, a young man lacking common sense,
walking at twilight down the street to the house of this
wayward girl, a prostitute. She approached him, saucy and pert,
and dressed seductively. She was the brash, coarse type, seen
often in the streets and markets, soliciting at every corner for
men to be her lovers.

She put her arms around him and kissed him, and with a
saucy look she said, "I was just coming to look for you and here
you are! Come home with me, and I'll fix you a wonderful dinner,
and after that—well, my bed is spread with lovely, colored sheets
of finest linen imported from Egypt, perfumed with myrrh, aloes,
and cinnamon. Come on, let's take our fill of love until morning,
for my husband is away on a long trip. He has taken a wallet full
of money with him and won't return for several days."

So she seduced him with her pretty speech, her coaxing and
her wheedling, until he yielded to her. He couldn't resist her
flattery. He followed her as an ox going to the butcher or as a
stag that is trapped, waiting to be killed with an arrow through
its heart. He was as a bird flying into a snare, not knowing the
fate awaiting it there.

Listen to me, young men, and not only listen but obey;
don't let your desires get out of hand; don't let yourself think
about her. Don't go near her; stay away from where she walks,
lest she tempt you and seduce you. For she has been the ruin of
multitudes—a vast host of men have been her victims. If you
want to find the road to hell, look for her house.

PROVERBS 7:6-27, TLB

This description of a foolish man entrapped by sexual temptation
strikes close to home for so many of us. It sends fear through our minds
about our own susceptibility. What can we do? How can we escape the
traps that appear before us?

Several guidelines for dealing with sexual temptations emerge from this passage:

1. Don't let your desires get out of hand. Control them.
2. Don't let yourself think about her. Guard your mind.
3. Don't go near her. Run from tempting circumstances.
4. Guard your eyes. Be careful what you see—movies, photographs, other women. "I made a covenant with my eyes not to look lustfully at a young woman" (Job 31:1).

Our marriages and our lives are at stake. We ought to fear the consequences, for they are great. We need to cut the temptation at its root to prevent its devouring impact on our lives.

You may be saying, "It's too late. I've already given in to sexual temptation. My marriage is broken or disintegrating. What do I do now?" God is a God of compassion and forgiveness. He can and will intervene if you give Him permission. He can rebuild what has been torn down. God is willing and ready to work on your behalf.

None of us can escape sexual temptation. It's a fact of life. And men who claim to follow Christ should want to live a life of purity. We cannot do it on our own. We need God's help to live a life of victory.

WHEN CONFLICT
BECOMES SIN

MEN ARE MADE "MORE FOR COMBAT than comfort," writes Elliot Engel in a *Newsweek* commentary on men's friendships.[1] Competition and conflict seem to suit men. Conflict is the norm in the business world. Conflict over ideas, strategies, concepts, methods, and decisions are part of every man's job experience.

We evaluate, discuss, and compromise. Some men handle this environment of competition for ideas very well, while others shrivel inwardly and develop ulcers.

When Conflict Becomes Dangerous

Conflict is normal within certain boundaries. Discussion, dialogue, and constructive criticism comprise positive elements of our conversations. But we can cross a boundary when emotions flare. Anger deepens, and personal tension enters relationships. Even then, conflict can be constructive. We may not have crossed the boundary, but if another person does, the tension mounts.

It's healthy to recognize conflict and deal with it. Unacknowledged and left to simmer, conflict poisons our lives.

When is conflict a sign of danger to a man?

- When the conflict is a repeated pattern in your life
- When many or most of the conflicts remain unresolved
- When you sense a pattern of unwillingness to be open to other positions or thinking

Men engage in conflict easily, but they find it difficult to resolve. Aggressive conflict is often a way of life in work and business. But when combative conflict causes harm to others, or when it carries over to our marriages and friendships, it becomes destructive.

Paul, the feisty apostle, encountered his own share of conflict:

I am afraid that when I come I may not find you as I want you to be, and you may not find me as you want me to be. I fear that there may be discord, jealousy, fits of rage, selfish ambition, slander, gossip, arrogance and disorder.
2 CORINTHIANS 12:20

Paul saw his own friends from Corinth in conflict—and in sin. He both warned them and encouraged them to be at peace. We know that conflict is a seedbed for a multitude of moral sins. As men, we cannot let conflict pollute and spoil us.

Roots of Conflict

Unhealthy conflict differs from simple disagreement, debate, or discussion in that it springs from a root of sin. "Whoever loves a quarrel loves sin" (Proverbs 17:19). The strongest language on such conflict comes in Paul's list in Galatians 5:19-21 of "the acts of the flesh," a list that includes "hatred, discord, jealousy, fits of rage, selfish ambition, dissensions, factions and envy." God takes such things very seriously. As Paul goes on to say, "I warn you, as I did before, that those who live like this will not inherit the kingdom of God" (Galatians 5:21).

Discord, dissension, and factions form the heart of unhealthy or destructive conflict. Unfortunately, such conflict comes so naturally to men. Robert Hicks says that being a warrior represents a major element of a man's character. Hicks associates the Hebrew term *gibbor* (often translated "warrior") with the "idea of gaining the upper hand" and says, "As men we war in business, in sports, in marriage, in our conversations, and with our political agendas."[2] The essence of this conflict is our seeking to *win*. We want precisely that—to be a warrior who wins. In the normal conduct of life, such a combative attitude quickly becomes tiresome and unpalatable.

Conflict is one of the prime evidences of sinful worldliness. As Paul says of the Corinthians, "You are still worldly. For since there is jealousy and quarreling among you, are you not worldly? Are you not acting like mere humans?" (1 Corinthians 3:3).

You may wonder why I include conflict as an unseen or unexpected danger. I do so because of its profoundly destructive power on individuals and communities. I also include it because it's so hard for a man to admit that he's wrong in a conflict or that conflict is a harmful pattern in his life. In marriage, unresolved conflict leads to great tension and opens the path to divorce. Conflict is at the root of most divorces.

Results of Conflict

The results of conflict for the individual man are manifold. Conflict leads to anger, both internal and external.

Individual conflict usually precedes group conflict. One person begins disagreeing with another. Then that personal conflict infects the entire group. Throughout the Bible, conflict and dissension caused murder, wars, division of families, and struggles for power.

In the church body, difficulties surface more often from interpersonal conflict and disagreements than from any differences over doctrine. When churches fail to grow and the lost are not being reached, at the root you'll find internal conflict among the leadership. Disagreement isn't wrong in itself, since we gain insight from differing perspectives. It becomes sin when it exceeds the boundary of grace and respect for others' views.

Conflict destroys friendships and working relationships. The Bible says, "An evil man sows strife; gossip separates the best of friends" (Proverbs 16:28, TLB). Unresolved conflict puts a wedge between friends. It prevents peace and unity, which are highly valued in Scripture. "If you bite and devour each other, watch out or you will be destroyed by each other" (Galatians 5:15). Prolonged conflict is the antithesis of love.

Conflict also causes spiritual weakness and immaturity. Isaiah wrote of the striking hypocrisy of practicing fasting while engaged in quarreling:

> For day after day they seek me out;
> > they seem eager to know my ways.
> > . . . eager for God to come near them. . . .
>
> Yet on the day of your fasting, you do as you please
> > and exploit all your workers.
> Your fasting ends in quarreling and strife,
> > and in striking each other with wicked fists.
> You cannot fast as you do today
> > and expect your voice to be heard on high.
>
> ISAIAH 58:2-4

In *The Living Bible*'s paraphrase of 1 Corinthians 3:3, this same truth is highlighted:

> You are still only baby Christians, controlled by your own desires, not God's. When you are jealous of one another and divide up into quarreling groups, doesn't that prove you are still babies, wanting your own way? In fact, you are acting like people who don't belong to the Lord at all.

Jesus instructs us to be reconciled with others before offering spiritual sacrifices since we cannot have intimate fellowship with God when we're in a state of conflict (Matthew 5:24).

The result of conflict in a community of believers is disunity and dissension. This is a sad witness to the nonbelieving world. Conflict in the Christian family leads to divisions and rifts that may last for a lifetime. Men and women everywhere are deeply wounded by such conflict.

The Way out of Conflict

Although it's true that it takes two or more people to engender open conflict, examine yourself to see if you often create and foster conflict.

What is the source of conflict? According to Proverbs 13:10, pride is one primary source. Our pride keeps us from admitting we're wrong. It keeps us from seeing other points of view.

Another source is sinful desires:

> What causes fights and quarrels among you? Don't they come
> from your desires that battle within you? You desire but do not
> have, so you kill. You covet but you cannot get what you want,
> so you quarrel and fight. You do not have because you do not
> ask God. When you ask, you do not receive, because you ask
> with wrong motives, that you may spend what you get on your
> pleasures.
>
> JAMES 4:1-3

The root of conflict is in our inner person—a selfishness and pride that offends God and others.

If you find this persistent pattern of conflict in your life, there is a way out. Here are good action steps you can take:

First, confess this pattern to God. He already knows it, but confession is an admission of your need and a cry for help to God. Men find it so difficult to admit need, even privately to God.

Next, identify the major unresolved conflicts in your life. Write them down. Putting them on a piece of paper brings a new reality to them. It's also a reminder for later when you may try to rationalize them away.

Begin a process of forgiveness and reconciliation. This will take time. You may need to forgive or be forgiven. David describes the relief of forgiveness in these words. "What happiness for those whose guilt has been forgiven! What joys when sins are covered over! What relief for those who have confessed their sins and God has cleared their record" (Psalm 32:1-2, TLB). In the following verses, David relates how silence can make us physically ill and how peace relieves when forgiveness is active. You, also, may need to either ask for or give forgiveness.

Reconciliation sometimes isn't easy. It's a process that takes two people, and it takes work and time. (I recommend Ken Sande's book *The Peacemaker: A Biblical Guide to Resolving Personal Conflict*. It outlines in detail how to bring about reconciliation. This topic is discussed further by Ken Sande, together with Kevin Johnson, in their book *Resolving Everyday Conflict*.)[3]

For the future, remember these words of biblical wisdom: "It is to one's honor to avoid strife, but every fool is quick to quarrel" (Proverbs 20:3). Simply avoiding strife is a key strategy. Knowing your tendencies, don't let yourself enter the conflict.

Remember also these wise words from Scripture: "Starting a quarrel is like breaching a dam; so drop the matter before a dispute breaks out" (Proverbs 17:14). As the old saying goes, "An ounce of prevention is worth a pound of cure." You cannot totally avoid or prevent conflict, but there's so much you *can* do to make sure you're not the instigator.

Also, ask God to deal with the root issues of pride and selfishness in your life. They're there for all of us. I find them constantly rearing their ugly heads in my own life. In my home, I find that pride and selfishness engender conflicts between Mary and me. I seem to control these issues better with others, but they're still there.

Some of us have never dealt with those root issues in a definitive way. It's a humbling but necessary experience. I've also found that I don't initiate dealing with them myself; rather, God takes His surgical knife and does it in a public and humbling way.

God simply will not tolerate our selfishness and pride for long. As we recognize this, we can confess first to God, and then to others. I remember the wife of one of our Navigator staff members who began this process at a staff conference. She shocked everyone by getting up and saying, "I have been an angry person all my life. I confess it to God and to you, and I want to change. If God can deliver me, he can deliver anybody." What a testimony! We were all deeply convicted.

Keep in mind, most of us enter conflict through our conversations with others. Thus we need to learn to guard our tongues—and our heart reactions. The biblical letter of James talks quite bluntly about the tongue:

> Those who consider themselves religious and yet do not keep a tight rein on their tongues deceive themselves, and their religion is worthless.
> JAMES 1:26

> The tongue is a small part of the body, but it makes great boasts. Consider what a great forest is set on fire by a small spark. The tongue also is a fire, a world of evil among the parts of the body. It corrupts the whole body, sets the whole course of one's life on fire, and is itself set on fire by hell.
> JAMES 3:5-6

We need to treat our tendency to be in conflict at two levels. The first level is what we say and how we say it. The second is our hearts and emotions. Our personalities often govern our reactions, but those reactions can be controlled and changed by God's work in our lives.

Finally, we need to take full responsibility for our own actions, doing all that we can to curb and cure conflict: "If it is possible, as far as it depends on you, live at peace with everyone" (Romans 12:18).

As men, we know that stress is one of the major contributors to health problems and that it affects our personal well-being. I believe that conflict is a major source of stress for many men. Whether we're the initiator or the receiver of conflict, the stress takes its toll. Let's pledge to do our best to moderate our tendency to be in conflict by turning conflicts into productive discussions laced with grace and respect.

12

WHEN ANGER
BECOMES SIN

I PLAY HANDBALL. Perhaps I should say I *still* play handball. That admission in itself (as I'm told by friends) is enough to commit me to some category of instability or craziness.

As in most competitive sports, in handball I see a lot of anger. Men slam their fists into the wall, swear at themselves, or argue over a shot or a foul. Usually, their temper is their undoing in a game. Only a very few play the game better when they're angry.

Most of us who play handball will tolerate some degree of anger in others and in ourselves. But there are some people with whom no one likes to play. Their hotheaded conduct on the court is unbearable and inexcusable. I've seen yelling matches that come just short of physical blows. Some players become sullen and give up, ruining the game by not playing to the best of their ability.

When the game is over, they leave in their business suits and go back to being a lawyer, teacher, engineer, businessman, or stockbroker— seemingly normal people.

Emotional boundaries exist even in a game. Frustration, anger, disappointment with oneself, and discouragement over errors are certainly legitimate reactions. But the line is crossed when anger overtakes and controls a person. It affects everyone on the court and even those watching the match. Angry outbursts cause the player to lose other people's respect, regardless of whether he wins or loses the game.

So it is in life. Anger, out of bounds or in excess, never brings a good result.

Certainly, anger is not just a male emotion. Men and women alike feel and express anger. But they typically handle it differently. In the ongoing discussion over the differences in men's and women's communication and expression of feelings, there's the repeated frustration that men don't express their emotions. Anger is the one emotion that men *do* consistently express. But rather than communicating early on that their anger is building, men usually express their anger explosively.

Conflict, anger, and pride are inextricably intertwined. I'm discussing them separately because they form a trilogy of dangers that subvert maturity, personal growth, and meaningful relationships. Although pride is frequently at the root of anger, other factors also contribute. Personality, family upbringing, age, life experience, and spiritual maturity all contribute to how we handle anger.

We all feel anger. If we didn't, we wouldn't be human. We've seen in our own experience how anger can be a normal, even healthy, response in some circumstances. Anger becomes harmful and dangerous when it's persistent, repeated, and unresolved. Anger has its place and levels in each one of us.

Let's think of unhealthy anger at three levels: misdirected anger, the gray middle road of anger, and explosive anger.

Misdirected Anger

If a man said he never became angry, I would ask if he was still alive. At some level, anger is a recurring element of an emotional life. I've never met a person who didn't get angry at some time.

I think I'm an example of a person who experiences some anger but rarely expresses it. Part of my way of handling anger results from my personality, part of it is from my training and experience over the years, and part of it is from the requirements of my job.

My family rarely sees me angry. In fact, that has been a hindrance to some of them. They've told me that I'm too emotionally level. They want me to become upset and angry on their behalf—for example, when a boyfriend mistreats them or they're treated unjustly. But I'm so much a "balancer" and "soother of conflict" that I tend to plead the other person's case.

In the few times when my anger has bubbled over, it actually frightened or intimidated people. My anger was never explosive but intense and obvious. As a result, I found I had to learn how I could handle it. Like many men, I generally subdue my anger rather than express it. The problem is that in doing so we may subdue many emotions, not just anger.

Most of us know when our anger is appropriate and within proper, biblical bounds. Anger about injustice, evil in our communities, or sin in our own lives is where it's appropriate. Anger in these cases can sharpen our thinking and resolve. It can galvanize us into action. It can thrust us into the role of protector and defender.

The rarity of my expression of anger does not mean that it is never a problem for a person like me. When I'm angry over not getting my way, or at others for not performing up to my expectations, or at my wife when we're in conflict, or at my children when they disobey, then I cross that line into sin. I may not express the anger inappropriately, but I know it's still there.

Usually when a man expresses his anger in an inappropriate or hurtful way, he feels almost immediate remorse and regret. That's when an apology is in order and should be given. There are many times when I've had to ask for forgiveness from my family and others.

Anger's Gray Middle Road

Even though not all anger is sin, some men find themselves getting angry far too often and expressing it more than they should. They don't fit the "angry man" profile, but they still sense their anger crossing that unhealthy boundary.

What's the evidence that you're walking this middle road of anger?

The first evidence is that you see it in yourself. Your conscience quickly registers the emotions of irritation turning to anger. You always have a chance to stop its progress. When you don't stop it, it either gets bottled up inside or bursts out in harsh words and actions. When it's consistently held inside, it can result in ulcers, depression, or discouragement. When it expresses itself naturally, it causes tension, conflict, and broken relationships. You may think, *There's no way to win with this anger.*

To hear your child say, "Daddy, why are you mad at me?" is a sad reminder that you crossed the line. The cool silence from your wife certainly tells you that something's wrong. You would never hit or hurt anyone physically, but you still sense that you crossed the boundary of normal irritation to anger that hurts yourself and others.

I've crossed this boundary at times myself—usually within the confines of my family. I didn't like having to ask forgiveness from my wife or children, but I found it necessary.

We may find ourselves being whispered about by people at work: "Don't talk to him today. He got up on the wrong side of the bed." Or you may not hear them say it, but you know you're grumpy, and you sense people staying away. Those are times when we don't know exactly what's best—to hide it or let it show. When we hide our irritation and anger, there's a good chance we can get to the root. So often, however, it just eats at us with no resolutions.

Explosive Anger

A few men have what I call "explosive anger." It's there inside, often surfacing to harm others emotionally and even physically at times.

Greg knew he had a problem with anger. It showed in his eyes, his posture, and his tone of voice. His father had been abusive, having beaten him regularly. His wife tried to pacify him and balance his extremes through the years. He had a son who was out of control, acting just as he did: exhibiting uncontrollable, explosive anger and engaging in violent behavior and verbal battles.

Greg was on the edge of physically abusing his wife. She ran. He pleaded and promised, as he had many times before, that he would change. He was a believer with a desire to walk with God. But an inner fire of anger controlled him. He finally became desperate enough to seek help.

He gave little indication in public of his volatile nature. Most people saw a capable man, intense, hardworking, and competitive.

So it is for some of us. The anger resides deep within us. Most of the time we control it. Occasionally it explodes within the family or during high-stress situations. Between explosions, we feel it simmering inwardly.

This explosive anger is destructive to ourselves, our children, our marriages, and our relationships. Some men feel helpless, knowing it's wrong but unable to control it. So often a man's family background or his peer environment as a young person stimulates and ignites this anger. But it's possible to get victory over it.

Each level of anger described here has a measure of sin. Clearly, explosive anger can cause the most damage. But the other types of anger also reflect issues of character that God wants to change in us.

The Bible's View of Unrighteous Anger

Three Scriptures capture the biblical view of unrighteous anger:

- Do not be quickly provoked in your spirit, for anger resides in the lap of fools. (Ecclesiastes 7:9)
- Fools give full vent to their rage, but the wise bring calm in the end. (Proverbs 29:11)
- An angry person stirs up conflict, and a hot-tempered person commits many sins. (Proverbs 29:22)

These are blunt statements. An angry man is a fool. A wise man controls anger. Anger causes conflict. Anger leads to sin—many sins.

The first murder in the Bible resulted from anger. Cain was angry with God, "very angry" (Genesis 4:5). God confronted him about his anger, identifying it as the attempt of Satan to destroy him. Cain went on to carry out his anger by murdering his brother Abel.

Other famous men of the Bible destroyed their lives by anger. Moses, the man who talked with God face-to-face, struck a rock in anger to get water for the people although God had instructed him to speak to the rock. In anger and frustration with the people, he said, "Listen, you rebels, must we bring you water out of this rock?" (Numbers 20:10). And then:

> Moses raised his arm and struck the rock twice with his staff. Water gushed out. . . .
>
> But the LORD said to Moses and Aaron, "Because you did not trust in me enough to honor me as holy in the sight of the Israelites, you will not bring this community into the land I give them."
>
> NUMBERS 20:11-12

Moses acted in anger and lost his dream. Note that he did not harm a person. He wasn't an angry man. Yet in a moment of crisis, he yielded to his anger.

Samson, the strong man who was a judge of Israel, lived a life of disastrous anger and lust. It finally killed him (see Judges 14:19, 16:30).

Anger often precedes sin. In Galatians 5:19-20, anger is described as "a fit of rage," appearing alongside sexual immorality, impurity, debauchery, idolatry, and witchcraft in a list of "the acts of the flesh." Anger poisons our physical and spiritual lives as well as our relationships. We cannot excuse anger by blaming personality or background.

What results when we fail to deal with anger in our lives? When anger boils out verbally or in outward attributes like sullenness, irritability, or other nonverbal signals easily recognized by family and friends, what happens is this:

- It causes tensions.
- It engenders conflict.
- It hurts those closest to us.
- It leaves us with guilt and regret.
- It breaks friendships.
- It ruins work relationships.
- It intimidates and frightens our children.

If you have explosive anger, you recognize these results all too well. It's especially damaging in the family. To see children cower in our presence should be enough to cause us to change. A little boy or girl should never have to question, "Am I safe around Daddy?" Whether or not our anger is resolved internally, it can devastate those around us.

Anger turned inward has these effects:

- It makes us physically ill (and can even give us ulcers).
- It derails spiritual growth.
- It affects our entire outlook on life.
- It robs us of joy.

Making a Change

So what do we do with anger? Whether we express it or internalize it, anger can be so damaging, yet it's still such a prominent part of many men's lives.

Several steps can be taken to effect permanent change in any pattern of anger you may see in yourself.

1. Admit to yourself that you have a problem with anger. Admit that it's sin. Recognize it as an offense against God (Ephesians 4:31). Confess it to God, asking for His forgiveness.

2. Share the problem with a close friend and ask him to hold you accountable for change. This will provide a place where you can talk through some of your feelings about your anger.

3. Ask for forgiveness from your wife, children, or others who are close to you. This is not an easy step. Tell them you want to change, and ask for both their patience and help.

4. With your close friends, discuss and write out what you perceive causes your anger. Possibilities are basic personality, habit patterns, not getting your way, pride, a shallow walk with God, not wanting to admit you're wrong, or fear of failure. You'll likely find one or two primary sources.

5. Ask God to change you. Make specific commitments for which you'll be held accountable. You may need the help of a biblically oriented counselor. Meanwhile, as one of my friends said, "Count to ten before you say anything."

You'll be amazed at the change you sense in your life and relationships.

I assure you that there's real hope. As discouraging as uncontrolled or misdirected anger can be, God has given us the promised fruit of the Spirit: love, joy, peace, longsuffering, gentleness, goodness, faith, meekness, and temperance (Galatians 5:22-23, KJV). And because of this truth, I've seen men change radically—both externally and internally. They move deeply into the peaceful reality of living out this instruction: "Be kind and compassionate to one another, forgiving each other, just as in Christ God forgave you" (Ephesians 4:32).

◆13◆

WHEN PRIDE
BECOMES SIN

EARLY IN MY AIR FORCE CAREER, I was stationed in Florida at Patrick Air Force Base, the headquarters for the Atlantic Missile Range and the Air Force Missile Test Center at Cape Canaveral. Mary and I were heavily involved in the base's chapel program. The pianist at the chapel was not very skilled. Reflecting on her feelings playing at the service for the first time, Mary recounts:

I had been critical of the skill of the person who had been playing the piano. When my turn came, I thought, *Wait until they hear how it really should be done.* The music that day went well, and I was feeling smug. Then in the silence during the pastoral prayer, the hymnbook fell from the music rack onto the piano keys, loudly disturbing the silence of the moment and shattering my pride. On the way home Jerry laughed; I cried all the way, embarrassed and humiliated. Yet it is one of the best lessons that could have happened to get at my pride.

A Life-Changing Experience

Being a mission controller at Cape Canaveral was a highlight of my life as well as life-changing in terms of my professional direction. I cannot help but think about how I got there.

When I entered the Air Force, I embarked on a year of pilot training. I was rather blasé about it all. I did reasonably well and was coasting along near the end of my year in the first phase of jet training in the T-33. In my formation check ride, I made an error during takeoff that allowed the nose wheel to become cocked on the power run-up at the end of the runway. This caused me to fall behind the lead aircraft about fifty yards as I lifted off. I got caught in the lead plane's jet wash, and the plane suddenly banked in a dangerous way. I was shaken!

The rest of the flight was a disaster. I failed miserably. On a recheck two days later, I flew reasonably well, but the check pilot simply said, "You can fly two-ship formation but not well enough to fly four-ship formation." Then he gave me a failing grade, and I was out of pilot training! No recourse.

Up to this point in my life, I hadn't failed in any significant way. Life had been one success after another. My pride was wounded. After all, why be in the Air Force if I couldn't fly? So I asked God—and the Air Force—to give me an engineering assignment anywhere. I planned to serve my mandatory three years and get out. God intervened, and through no effort on my part, He put me in the midst of the new space program. I couldn't have planned it better. But first God had to wound my pride. I wish I could say it was broken, but it was not. There was much to come in my life that would cause me to deal with my prideful spirit.

The Motives of the Heart

Writing a chapter on pride is rather difficult. I feel hypocritical, since I see so many issues of pride in my life. I've chosen to use primarily my own personal illustrations (or Mary's, with her permission). I feel it's virtually impossible to discern whether someone else is being prideful. Pride is more a motive of the heart than it is an action. One man may appear prideful but does not have prideful motives. Another man may appear humble yet be driven by intense pride. I find it difficult to know exactly when I'm being motivated by pride.

Paul correctly describes this dilemma:

> I care very little if I am judged by you or by any human court; indeed, I do not even judge myself. My conscience is clear, but that does not make me innocent. It is the Lord who judges me. Therefore judge nothing before the appointed time; wait until the Lord comes. He will bring to light what is hidden in darkness and will expose the motives of the heart.
>
> I CORINTHIANS 4:3-5

Only God really knows our motives fully.

Oswald Chambers writes the following about conceit (or pride):

> We have to get rid of the idea that we understand ourselves, it is the last conceit to go. The only One Who understands us is God. The greatest curse in spiritual life is conceit. If we have ever had a glimpse of what we are like in the sight of God, we shall never say—"Oh, I am so unworthy" because we shall know we are, beyond the possibility of stating it. . . . Whenever there is any element of pride or of conceit, Jesus cannot expound a thing. He will take us through the disappointment of a wounded pride of intellect, through disappointments of heart.[1]

It seems that heartbreak and disappointment are the primary means that God uses to break the bonds of pride in our lives. I wonder why it's so hard? Why can't we just decide to be humble? The root is the sinful nature that still tries to control us.

God's View of Pride

God doesn't mince words in His view of pride. "Whoever has haughty eyes and a proud heart, I will not tolerate" (Psalm 101:5); "I hate pride and arrogance, evil behavior and perverse speech" (Proverbs 8:13). The message is simple. God will not tolerate pride. He'll do whatever He must to dig it out at the roots. (One book that has been a help to me on this is *Embracing Brokenness* by Alan E. Nelson.)[2]

Pride is the most subtle of all the dangers. Most of us fail to recognize its power over us, as well as the constancy of the battle required to resist it. We may start to sense it but then ignore it. We become used to pride's presence and excuse its evilness as a friend to be tolerated. We rebuke it, and it recedes temporarily, only to appear again in a different suit of clothes. We disdain its hold on us yet feel insecure and undressed without it. Such is pride—slippery and elusive, deadly and destructive.

In our more spiritual moments we might say, "How could anyone tolerate sinful pride?" as though there were any other kind. It comes in such attractive and compelling forms: pride of person, success, possession, and position.

Pride of person portends to take credit for who we are. Our intellect, race, abilities, appearance, and upbringing each demand a place in our pride. Yet we had, and have, no control over any of them. "What do you have that you did not receive?" (1 Corinthians 4:7) is drowned out by "Look at me! Aren't I *something*!" All that we have in our person is from God, by His grace. We did nothing to earn it.

But we can do much to spoil it. We're commanded to be thankful for our heritage and the sovereign creation of our person. We care for this creation. We respect and value it in ourselves and others. God deeply values us as His creation. But we cannot take credit for it. Pride has no just foundation here.

Every man wants to be a success and to achieve and accomplish. This is normal and right. God made us that way. The problem arises when we take the credit.

One King's Pride

Babylon, fifty-five miles south of modern Baghdad in what's now the country of Iraq, was once the greatest city of its time, in the seventh and sixth centuries BC. With a population of one hundred thousand and boasting over eleven hundred temples, Babylon was surrounded by triple walls having a circumference of forty-two miles. Inside were its famous Hanging Gardens, one of the seven wonders of the ancient world. The city stood on the banks of the Euphrates River, rising on a plain that in more ancient times was possibly the site of the famous tower of Babel. Babylon's ruins still stand as a silent testimony to past splendor.

Nebuchadnezzar II reigned as king of the Babylonian Empire from 605 to 562 BC. During his father's reign, he was a brilliant military strategist, leading the historic victory over the Egyptians at Carchemish in 605 BC. That victory established Babylonian authority over all western Asia, thus ranking it as one of the most decisive battles of all time.

Nebuchadnezzar built the Hanging Gardens and most of Babylon, making it a place of incredible beauty and splendor. He was a great and brilliant king.

One of Nebuchadnezzar's key advisers was a Jewish captive named Daniel. At one point, Nebuchadnezzar had a strange dream that only Daniel was able to interpret. Daniel was terrified by the dream, since it predicted disaster for a king who had achieved such glorious heights:

> You have become great and strong; your greatness has grown until it reaches the sky, and your dominion extends to distant parts of the earth. . . .
> This is the decree the Most High has issued against my lord the king: You will be driven away from people and will live with the wild animals; you will eat grass like the ox and be drenched with the dew of heaven.
> DANIEL 4:22, 24-25

Wanting the king to avoid this disaster, Daniel gave him this counsel:

Therefore, Your Majesty, be pleased to accept my advice:
Renounce your sins by doing what is right, and your
wickedness by being kind to the oppressed. It may be that then
your prosperity will continue.

DANIEL 4:27

Twelve months later, Nebuchadnezzar stood on the roof of his palace
in Babylon looking over the great city.

"Is not this the great Babylon I have built as the royal residence,
by my mighty power and for the glory of my majesty?"
    Even as the words were on his lips, a voice came from
heaven, "This is what is decreed for you, King Nebuchadnezzar:
Your royal authority has been taken from you. You will be
driven away from people and will live with the wild animals;
you will eat grass like the ox. Seven times will pass by for you
until you acknowledge that the Most High is sovereign over all
kingdoms on earth and gives them to anyone he wishes."

DANIEL 4:30-32

What the heavenly voice decreed is what immediately happened.
    Later, Nebuchadnezzar's son (or possibly grandson) Belshazzar
became king. Daniel, now an old man, was called to interpret hand-
writing that appeared on the wall during a drunken feast. Daniel spoke
to Belshazzar these words about Nebuchadnezzar: "When his heart
became arrogant and hardened with pride, he was deposed from his
royal throne and stripped of his glory" (Daniel 5:20).

Honoring God in Our Success

The message is clear: God will not tolerate our arrogance or our pride in
our success or achievements. We may receive honor, but we must give
the honor to God.
    That's easy to say, but not so easy to do in our hearts. Somehow we

still think that we achieved it on our own. But we've simply been using the gifts God gave us to do what He wanted.

Whether in business, education, craftsmanship, speaking, or earning money, success is from God. Any success can be reversed in a moment, so we dare not become proud. "Pride brings a person low" (Proverbs 29:23).

Possessions and wealth can easily make a person proud. We see it daily. Wealth is relative. Wealthy compared to whom? Each of us has more possessions and is wealthier than someone else. It's all a matter of perspective. It seems that the amount matters little.

One man has an extra pickup truck and a small fishing boat in addition to his house, and he feels like he has a lot. Another man has three cars, a house on the lake, and a larger one in the city, yet he always strives to get more. What is important is how we view our possessions, not how much we have.

The Scriptures are filled with teaching and warning on money and possessions. "Those who trust in their riches will fall, but the righteous will thrive like a green leaf" (Proverbs 11:28). "Watch out! Be on your guard against all kinds of greed; life does not consist in an abundance of possessions" (Luke 12:15).

Pride in possessions can be a subtle trap. We may get so used to having nice things—a good home or an excess of money—that we forget what it was like not to have them, and we grow to expect them as a right.

The worst kind of pride comes when we look down on others who don't have much. I've noticed how people avoid men who are unemployed. Some jobless men have told me it's as if they'd become a leper.

Wealth and possessions are so temporary that it's amazing how much we depend on them. Scripture tells us,

> Do not wear yourself out to get rich;
>   do not trust your own cleverness.
> Cast but a glance at riches, and they are gone,
>   for they will surely sprout wings
>   and fly off to the sky like an eagle.
>
> PROVERBS 23:4-5

And,

> Whoever loves money never has enough;
> whoever loves wealth is never satisfied with their income.
> This too is meaningless.
>
> ECCLESIASTES 5:10

Biblical Instruction on Wealth

The most basic instruction on wealth and possessions is in the New Testament outline of the attitude God desires:

> Keep your lives free from the love of money and be content with what you have, because God has said, "Never will I leave you; never will I forsake you."
>
> HEBREWS 13:5

> For we brought nothing into the world, and we can take nothing out of it. But if we have food and clothing, we will be content with that. Those who want to get rich fall into temptation and a trap and into many foolish and harmful desires that plunge people into ruin and destruction. For the love of money is a root of all kinds of evil. Some people, eager for money, have wandered from the faith and pierced themselves with many griefs. . . .
> Command those who are rich in this present world not to be arrogant nor to put their hope in wealth, which is so uncertain, but to put their hope in God, who richly provides us with everything for our enjoyment. Command them to do good, to be rich in good deeds, and to be generous and willing to share. In this way they will lay up treasure for themselves as a firm foundation for the coming age, so that they may take hold of the life that is truly life.
>
> I TIMOTHY 6:7-10, 17-19

Life that is truly life—it's what we all want. But it doesn't come as a result of wealth. We must resist any pride that wells up in us regarding our possessions, which are only temporary. Yet we're taught that we can enjoy them freely as from God. When we do possess much, we can be generous. Generosity is an expression of gratefulness and humility. It's a privilege to meet others' needs, to help widows and orphans, to fund efforts to bring the gospel to a hurting world. When we accumulate wealth, we inherit great responsibility to use it well. (David Green, founder of Hobby Lobby, helpfully discusses this in his book *Giving It All Away*.)[3]

Pride of Position

Finally, consider pride of position. I discussed much of this in chapter 4 on loss of position. Pride of position in your work, your society, your neighborhood, or your church can quietly invade your mind. *Do they know who I am? If they knew, they would treat me better.*

Sad to say, this comes up in my own life far more frequently than I would wish. Every time I think of using the title *doctor* or *general*, I'm filled with a question of pride. I silently want people to know.

Any position is temporary. And all positions are from God, to be used for His glory.

The Consequences of Pride

When we allow pride a place in our lives, what results can we expect?

- *It will cause us to fall.* "Pride goes before destruction, a haughty spirit before a fall" (Proverbs 16:18).

- *It will put us in danger of God's anger.* "The LORD detests all the proud of heart. Be sure of this: They will not go unpunished" (Proverbs 16:5).

- *It will bring disgrace.* "When pride comes, then comes disgrace, but with humility comes wisdom" (Proverbs 11:2).

- *It will engender conflict.* "Where there is strife, there is pride" (Proverbs 13:10).

The antithesis of pride is humility. It's a character trait that God greatly honors. "All of you, clothe yourselves with humility toward one another" (1 Peter 5:5). Then, as the passage goes on to state, God will exalt or promote us in His good timing.

How is humility built? Usually through suffering. When our son was murdered, I found that so much of what I'd been prideful about didn't matter at all. My outlook on what was important changed dramatically. But even in that terrible time, I saw pride rearing its ugly head.

Larry Crabb, in his book *Finding God*, reflects this idea:

> Within days of my brother's death, I spoke at his memorial service. As I prepared my few comments on behalf of our family, I prayed that God would use my stumbling tongue in this difficult situation to encourage others to trust in the goodness of God no matter what might happen in their lives. I wanted to give.
>
> At one point during my talk, I noticed that a phrase I had just used was especially rich. As any experienced public speaker might do, I paused to let that phrase sink in. During that three-second pause, I heard these words run through my mind, "I'm doing a pretty good job. That was a good pause." Immediately, I felt slapped in the face by the realization that at that moment I cared more about how I was performing than about how meaningfully I was ministering.
>
> That night I wept bitterly. I grieved that even at my brother's funeral I couldn't escape the wretched power of pride.[4]

So we struggle to remove that root of pride that so deeply offends God and causes us to sin.

For all people, pride is a constant. Whether subtle and hidden or blatant and obvious, it permeates too much of our lives. Therefore, so much of our spiritual growth is tied to replacing this pride with Christlike humility. We desperately need the instruction from the apostle Peter (who knew quite a lot about pride): "Humble yourselves, therefore, under God's mighty hand, that he may lift you up in due time" (1 Peter 5:6).

Is there any antidote for these sinful dangers—sexual temptation, uncontrolled anger, combative conflict, and pride? We now turn to such a possibility.

14

THE ANTIDOTE FOR SIN

AFTER MARY'S CANCER WAS DISCOVERED, she had radiation therapy appointments at the same time that a dear friend and the wife of one of the Navigator staff members was receiving similar treatment. Two years later, our friend died, and Mary is cancer free, to the best of our knowledge. We reflected that Mary could also have been taken in death.

From a spiritual perspective, we know God is sovereign. From a human perspective, several issues clearly emerge.

Anyone who has had cancer intimately knows the critical factors. Early detection. Immediate action. Attempt at complete removal and eradication. Preventive treatment for recurrence.

Mary's cancer was completely removed surgically, with preventive treatment to follow. Our friend's cancer could not be completely erased.

Sin is a cancer of the soul. It intrudes and destroys. It resists detection and treatment. It is persistent and devious.

Principles for the Detection of the Cancer of Sin

If only sin could simply be detected and removed! Yet the principles for eradicating sin are similar to the treatment of cancer.

Early Detection

Procrastination is a terrible habit. It keeps us in bondage to all the undone tasks of our lives. Procrastination of certain cancer-detecting tests often costs lives. We all know that Pap tests and breast exams for women and prostate checks for men are a must. One of my handball friends didn't get his PSA checked for two years. His prostate cancer was found too late, resulting in his death. I found my prostate cancer early, and it was treated and removed.

Procrastination regarding sin is just as disastrous. The longer we allow the poison to remain in our lives, the more damage it will do. Ask God to reveal specific areas of sin to you. Look for it. Detect it early, before it gets a lifelong grip on you. Pray as David did: "Search me, God, and know my heart; test me and know my anxious thoughts. See if there is any offensive way in me, and lead me in the way everlasting" (Psalm 139:23-24). When you ask God to do this for you, He will. Once you've recognized and admitted to yourself that you've sinned, you can get an antidote working.

David went through this process regarding his adultery with Bathsheba in Psalm 51, where he said, "I know my transgressions, and my sin is always before me" (verse 3). David was fully conscious of his need.

Immediate Action

Listen to these words of pleading throughout David's prayer in Psalm 51:

> Cleanse me with hyssop, and I will be clean;
>   wash me, and I will be whiter than snow.
> Let me hear joy and gladness;
>   let the bones you have crushed rejoice. (51:7-8)

> Create in me a pure heart, O God,
>   and renew a steadfast spirit within me. (51:10)

> Restore to me the joy of your salvation
>   and grant me a willing spirit, to sustain me. (51:12)

David knew he had to be proactive in confessing his sin and seeking God's forgiveness. His words here convey a sense of urgency, an urgency no doubt quickened by the emotional suffering that immediately struck him once he was made conscious of his sin through the words of his friend Nathan, who held David accountable.

The longer we wait to take corrective action, the more difficult it becomes to do so. Like David, we feel unclean, we lack joy, and we feel crushed. We need to let that drive us to take action and to take full ownership of our sin.

Confession

What first action is required regarding sin? It is *confession*.

Confession is openly admitting our sins to God. "If we confess our sins, he is faithful and just and will forgive us our sins and purify us from all unrighteousness" (1 John 1:9).

To confess means to admit our guilt, to assent to God's sovereign standards, and to agree with God that our actions are unacceptable. Repentance is then turning from our sin. The confession itself results in forgiveness, which restores our fellowship with God. It is not about gaining salvation. Our salvation is assured if we've received Christ as Savior. But we also don't confess with the inner thought that we can sin in the same way again. We need the mindset that we will stop that sinful habit, action, or thought. In the Roman Catholic tradition, confession is more structured and engages a priest. But Roman Catholic doctrine clearly states that only God forgives. Confession to a priest and the act of penance is part of that process. But for all believers repentance must follow confession.

Confession is not trivial or just a quick naming of the sin. It's a deep admission of an offense to God. Nor is it, "Oh, I've been caught, so I might as well admit it." Rather, it's the sense that David expressed in prayer to God: "Against you, you only, have I sinned and done what is evil in your sight" (Psalm 51:4). A deep spirit of contrition accompanies confession. There is real remorse over our sin.

What about Uriah and Bathsheba? Didn't David sin against them? Yes, but his confession is primarily to God. He would live with and pay for his sin the rest of his life. And so might we, for our sins. Did David ask forgiveness of Bathsheba? We don't know from Scripture, but I assume he did.

Sin damages us and others deeply and often permanently. Confession may need to be offered to other people, depending on the nature of the sin. Ongoing relationship may require restoration and reconciliation. But another step must precede this.

Complete Removal

Just as cancer must be completely removed to render it ineffective, sin must be completely eradicated. With confession, our sin is immediately removed in terms of our relationship with God. Sin is forgiven, and we are cleansed. The Lord removed the eternal penalty from us when we first became a believer. The door for fellowship with God is opened again with confession.

However, recurrence of sin is not precluded. Some preventive measures need to be taken. It's not at all uncommon for a certain sin to persist and to discourage us with its reappearance. Thus, confession needs to be accompanied by repentance. One might argue that it's impossible to completely remove sin, especially sins that are more like addictions. True deliverance *is* possible—but may require counseling and accountability.

Repentance

Repentance is a conscious attitude of regret, a changing of our minds about our sin, and a turning from sin to God. This involves a reorientation to God.

In Greek, the noun *metanoia* ("repentance") and the related verb *metanoeō* ("to repent") refer to a change of mind or thinking differently—a reversal of sorts.

Repentance is active, as John the Baptist expressed in his preaching: "Produce fruit in keeping with repentance" (Luke 3:8).

The apostle Peter, on the day of Pentecost, showed us the sequence for and the results of repentance: "Repent, then, and turn to God, so that your sins may be wiped out, that times of refreshing may come from the Lord" (Acts 3:19).

The apostle Paul tied repentance to our actions as he summarized his consistent ministry to people everywhere: "I preached that they should repent and turn to God and demonstrate their repentance by their deeds" (Acts 26:20).

We don't repent with our fingers crossed, indicating that we don't really mean it. Real change is required. And change demands effort. The confession spoken of by the apostle John in 1 John 1:9 implies and even demands repentance. The two go hand in hand.

Does this mean that after you repent, you'll never commit this sin again? Not necessarily. But the intent of your heart must be that you will not. You now need the power of the Holy Spirit to keep your pledge of repentance.

A Christian leader told of his ten-year bondage to the sin of lust, which included a regular diet of pornography. During this time, he was conducting Christian conferences and seminars across the country. The agony of his inner conflict finally became unbearable. To his horror, he realized one day that pleasures such as a breathtaking sunset or the soft spray of an ocean breeze no longer excited him. His obsession with lust had dulled his appreciation of life's finest enjoyments and prevented the joy of fellowship with Jesus. Outwardly he'd been faithful to his wife, not having engaged in adultery. Yet he'd sinned against her, and their relationship had suffered.

When he turned anew to God, he realized that a necessary step in the breaking of his lustful pattern was a long talk with his wife. The whole experience was painful and awkward, but the repentance was genuine. She forgave him, and new love soon returned to their marriage.

C. S. Lewis said, "A Christian is not a man who never goes wrong, but a man who is enabled to repent and pick himself up and begin over again after each stumble—because the Christ-life is inside him, repairing him all the time."[1] Repentance requires action. Words simply prayed are not sufficient. Repentance involves true sorrow for sin.

After Paul wrote to confront believers in Corinth with their terrible moral and relational sins, he acknowledged in a later letter how those believers responded:

> Even if I caused you sorrow by my letter, I do not regret it. Though I did regret it—I see that my letter hurt you, but only for a little while—yet now I am happy, not because you were made sorry, but because *your sorrow led you to repentance*. For you became sorrowful as God intended. . . . Godly sorrow brings repentance that leads to salvation and leaves no regret, but worldly sorrow brings death.
>
> 2 CORINTHIANS 7:8-10, EMPHASIS ADDED

Navigator leader Mike Jordahl has shared that Jesus died not just for our sins but also for our sorrows. "Surely our griefs He Himself bore, and our sorrows He carried" (Isaiah 53:4, NASB). This prophecy points to Jesus.

True repentance produces a deep sense of having offended a holy God, a sorrow that is God-induced. Worldly sorrow is being sorry for getting caught or having hurt someone, but it lacks the dimension of knowing you've deeply offended God.

The human result of confession and repentance is a tremendous feeling of being clean. It's a new lease on life. Paul describes it this way:

> And now, isn't it wonderful all the ways in which this distress has goaded you closer to God? You're more alive, more concerned, more sensitive, more reverent, more human, more passionate, more responsible. Looked at from any angle, you've come out of this with purity of heart.
>
> 2 CORINTHIANS 7:11, MSG

That is what we want—purity of heart. What greater result of cleansing is there than purity of heart and peace of mind?

A Choice

When my children were growing up, a favorite statement of theirs after being corrected was this: "Dad! Nobody's perfect!" So true. None of us can ever say with 100 percent confidence, "I'll never do that again." We're fallen men in a fallen world, a world of sin and temptation.

Accountability is an essential part of prevention, but there's something even more important than that. God has made provision for us to overcome sin. Continuing our earlier discussion, we recall that God, in Christ, has paid the penalty for sin once and for all, and yet, sins (plural) still invade our lives.

In regard to this, Paul's teaching in Romans 6:12-13 stands out. He tells us:

> Do not let sin reign in your mortal body so that you obey
> its evil desires. Do not offer any part of yourself to sin as an
> instrument of wickedness, but rather offer yourselves to God
> as those who have been brought from death to life; and offer
> every part of yourself to him as an instrument of righteousness.

These words say that we must choose to not offer ourselves to sin. We have the power to make this choice because of Paul's next statement, which is a promise:

> For sin shall no longer be your master, because you are not
> under the law, but under grace.
> ROMANS 6:14

The death of the old self doesn't make us sinless, but it gives us the freedom and the power to *choose* whether we serve sin or serve righteousness. Before our salvation, we had no choice. Now we do.

We choose to refuse to let sin reign over us—to control us. Our human nature still responds to the temptation to sin, but we choose to resist it by our wills and by the power of the Holy Spirit (Romans 8:4-8; Galatians 5:16-25).

A Path for Righteous Living

Most believing men I know truly want to live a life that honors God. In the Gospels, Jesus gives us a number of commands to help us walk this path of righteous living:

1. "Come to me" (Matthew 11:28-30). When we come to Him, He equips us. He leads us. But He gives us the option to come voluntarily.

2. "Follow me" (John 12:25-26). We follow Him by giving up our right to live life on our terms. A believer can be described as "a follower of Christ." As we follow Him, we learn from Him. We experience His companionship and receive His guidance.

3. "Seek first his kingdom and his righteousness" (Matthew 6:33). This is giving God the first priority in our lives. *Seeking* implies that it requires effort to put Christ and His Kingdom first in our decisions. This command is given amid a discussion of the need for material and physical things. This seeking ought to be our daily goal.

4. Jesus also teaches us to go deep with God (Luke 6:48). The familiar story of a house built on rock shows that when we spend time with God daily, study His Word, and put it into practice, we're building a foundation that will endure the incessant trials of life and the invasion of sin. Poor foundations make for weak buildings.

5. He tells us to keep alert and keep going (Matthew 26:41). Vigilance against sin is a necessity. We cannot rest on our past purity. There's no assurance of holiness like there is an assurance of salvation. The flesh is weak. Only through the power of the Holy Spirit can we keep walking righteously.

6. Finally, Jesus commands us to go and proclaim the gospel (Matthew 28:18-20). A life committed to telling people about Christ and His love will help us avoid sin. As I travel, I do get

tempted in many ways. When I'm tempted in an airport book-
store, my commitment to share the gospel helps me resist pick-
ing up books or magazines that aren't holy or healthy. I often
have conversations with people in airports or airplanes. What if
they saw me violating what they know should be my standards?

Human Accountability

We nurture a life pattern of preventing sin by keeping close to God.
But there's also a human element of accountability. One of the things
that keeps me pursuing God and turning from sin is an accountability
relationship with three other men.

Although several of us had been friends for a number of years, in
1988 we decided to formalize our covenant and our commitment to
being accountable to one another. Our basic purpose is not simply to
help one another avoid sinning but also to keep one another faithful in
our walk with Jesus for a lifetime.

One of the men, Doug Hignell, recalled his initial reaction to this
idea: "Humble myself enough to be accountable to another person? Not
me, a man who likes to be in control and paddle his own canoe!" Those
words of Doug would have been my own response at one time.

Doug went on to say:

But as I began to grow in my spiritual walk, and as God
brought men with spiritual depth into my life, being a lone
ranger became less attractive. I began to realize that to remain
teachable as I got older and to end well in my Christian walk, I
needed to develop one or more relationships that would require
me to keep open and vulnerable.[2]

Doug, Stan, Chris, and I have made this covenant to help each other
finish well. Our wives have also made this covenant with us and with one
another. We've given one another full permission to invade each other's
lives, to ask any questions.

- A friend loves at all times, and a brother is born for a time of adversity. (Proverbs 17:17)
- Carry each other's burdens, and in this way you will fulfill the law of Christ. (Galatians 6:2)

This is what the four of us try to do for one another.

We desperately need one another. Unfortunately, no amount of accountability will keep a person from sin if he sets his mind on sinning. Accountability inhibits sin; it does not prevent it. The best accountability is not where men who are acquaintances get together with a list of questions, although that can be helpful as a minimum inhibitor. The best accountability is with close friends who know each other so well that they will sense when something's going astray and will say so. If, however, you don't open up your life, no one will invade it, even in a crisis.

The one downside to accountability in a close friendship is that a close friend can assume too much. He also may fear losing your friendship if he becomes suspicious and aggressively asks questions. We want to think the best of people. It's best to have accountability in a group setting with two or more close friends.

The prophet Nathan was King David's friend. Knowing the power of ancient Near Eastern kings, he risked his life as well as his friendship with David in confronting him about his sin with Bathsheba (2 Samuel 12:1-14).

Accountability doesn't necessarily need to be two-way. If you need it, seek it out. In his excellent book *The Man in the Mirror*, Patrick Morley defines accountability as being regularly answerable to qualified people for each of the key areas of our lives.[3]

Morley also includes what he calls the iceberg illustration. On the surface are casual conversations on sports, politics, weather, etc. Below the surface lurk the real issues: secret thoughts, ambitions, motives, marriage issues, moral and ethical behavior, relationships with God and others, use of time and money, the past, and much more.[4]

No one goes below the surface immediately. But the goal is to reveal what's below the surface of your life. "Make this your common practice: Confess your sins to each other and pray for each other so that you can live together whole and healed" (James 5:16, MSG).

Without accountability, we're very much alone. Then sin will isolate us even more:

Two are better than one,
     because they have a good return for their labor:
If either of them falls down,
     one can help the other up.
But pity anyone who falls
     and has no one to help them up. . . .
Though one may be overpowered,
     two can defend themselves.
A cord of three strands is not quickly broken.

ECCLESIASTES 4:9-12

The letter I wrote in chapter 10 gives a few ideas on what to ask in an accountability setting. Morley also gives an excellent accountability checkup list in *The Man in the Mirror.*[5]

Restoration, Reconciliation, and Restitution

The following three Rs must accompany confession of sin for full healing to occur. Consider carefully each one:

Restoration

Restoration means bringing back to the original or former condition. If you've sinned against a friend, the friendship needs restoration. When God forgives us, we're restored to fellowship with Him.

When Jesus healed a withered hand or a blind eye, the Bible says He restored them. In Galatians 6:1, the apostle Paul explains that when a person sins, we're to "restore that person gently."

Reconciliation

Reconciliation means to bring about harmony, agreement, or a settlement—to make peace when parties have been at variance with each other.

We're reconciled to God by the blood of Jesus Christ. When there are conflicts and offenses in our relationships with others, we're to be reconciled or brought into harmony before we can worship:

> If you are offering your gift at the altar and there remember
> that your brother or sister has something against you, leave
> your gift there in front of the altar. First go and be reconciled
> to them; then come and offer your gift.
>
> MATTHEW 5:23-24

Restitution

Restitution is compensation for a wrong done, the repayment of a debt, or redress for harm done. It's returning what has wrongfully been taken.

Throughout the Bible, restitution is promoted. A sign of righteousness and justice is to pay back whatever is taken, stolen, lost, or damaged. When Zacchaeus encountered Jesus, in Luke 19:1-10, his response was, "If I have cheated anybody out of anything, I will pay back four times the amount" (Luke 19:8).

After sinning, we have an obligation to make things right with the people we've sinned against. Even though we cannot force anyone to respond favorably to our attempts at restoration and reconciliation, we're obligated to try to reconcile. "If it is possible, as far as it depends on you, live at peace with everyone" (Romans 12:18).

Some business agreements may need healing if one party has failed to live up to the agreed obligations. If there's any question in your mind, make it right.

Restoration is something we can do from our side only. For instance, if you're divorced, you may need to review your obligation to your children and your former wife.

Restoration and reconciliation are similar and often go hand in hand. However, one can restore a relationship while still not reconciling an issue. We can agree to disagree. That often happens in marriage.

A Christian wife had a brief affair, and her youngest child was the result of that illicit relationship. She concealed it from her husband, and her guilt began to drive her crazy. Finally, unable to face her husband each day, she asked him to move out of the house.

When the woman came for counseling, she was distraught. When she was told that she needed to confess her sin to God and to her husband, she hesitated, but soon was on her knees before the Lord.

A little later, she confessed to her husband, who was also a Christian. As she started to ask for his forgiveness, he took her in his arms and said, "I forgive you. And I love our little boy just as much as if he came from me."

Today that family is living for the Lord. This would not have been the case if she had refused to humble herself, repent, and confess her sin.

Healing

If we have cancer, we want to be healed. That's the goal. We go through all the steps—identification, action, removal, treatment, and prevention—to be healed and become free of cancer. Of course, as many of us can testify from personal experience, cancer isn't always eradicated.

All sinners desire to be healed, to be free from the burden of the sins that have bound us. We know God forgives—but does He also heal?

Healing comes from God. It's a result of obedience. Forgiveness is instantaneous, but healing is usually a process. Even when we confess and repent, our emotions don't immediately catch up, particularly if our sin requires that we tell others or make attempts at reconciliation.

One of the main ingredients for healing is time, as implied in these Old Testament words:

Come, let us return to the LORD.
He has torn us to pieces
  but he will heal us;
he has injured us
  but he will bind up our wounds.
After two days he will revive us;
  on the third day he will restore us,
  that we may live in his presence.
Let us acknowledge the LORD;
  let us press on to acknowledge him.
As surely as the sun rises,
  he will appear;
he will come to us like the winter rains,
  like the spring rains that water the earth.

HOSEA 6:1-3

We ourselves need time, but others also need time for healing, since our sin has impacted them. Then we follow through with repentance, restoration, reconciliation, and restitution, allowing God and His Spirit to minister to us.

"He heals the brokenhearted and binds up their wounds" (Psalm 147:3). God is the healer. This promise of healing is to the brokenhearted. Sin breaks God's heart, and it should break ours when we sin. This is reflected in David's confession: "The sacrifices of God are a broken spirit; a broken and contrite heart, O God, You will not despise" (Psalm 51:17, NASB). The context of this statement is David's desire to offer a sacrifice to atone for his sin. But what God wanted was a broken spirit.

David's desire was to be restored to the joy of God's salvation, to be healed and at peace. That needs to be our desire too. Pray for a broken heart over sin.

God has an antidote for each of our sins. But like physical antidotes in the medical world, this antidote is worthless and ineffective until taken and applied. A physician may prescribe the medicine. We may buy it and set it on the bedroom dresser. But until it's taken, it has no healing effect.

In our spiritual lives, when we act in humility and in obedience to the One who died for us, we can live—really *live*, not just stumble through life without joy, burdened under persistent guilt. God wants us to experience this kind of peace that surpasses all human understanding.

PART THREE

More Dangers

THE DANGER OF FREEZING

POLITICIANS, PREACHERS, and corporate executives consistently present us with visions of change. Meanwhile, inside us, the inner debate about whether to change is manifested in two voices. The first voice decries the change, calling for a return to life in the past. A second voice promotes change with dire warnings of disaster if we don't embrace it.

I could easily list the revolutionary changes taking place all around us in computer technology, communication, workplace dynamics, or science, but change happens so rapidly, the list would be immediately obsolete. We reel not only from the changes themselves but also from the accelerating rate of change. We wish life would slow down so we could catch our breath.

Do you remember some of the relics of your past that have become obsolete? When I studied engineering, the slide rule was the key tool of my trade. Now slide rules are museum pieces. Clothing styles and hairdos mark the decades. Our media instruments keep changing as technology changes. Telephones have radically evolved (and continue to do so) in the digital age. We admire classic cars, but we want to drive the latest technological wonder on four wheels.

As men grow older, many of them finally come to a place where they refuse to keep changing. There's comfort in the old and familiar. The old computer will do just fine. We can resist change and refuse to adapt, but then we'll be isolated and out of touch. Such resistance may be especially noticeable in the elderly, but it can also permeate the mind of every person who's mentally and emotionally overloaded with change.

You can draw your own picture of people you know who seem to have frozen in time. They set and harden like concrete, unable to change.

You might say, "What's wrong with that? Being an up-to-date fashion plate is not of high value." That's true. What does matter is whether a man's thinking, perspectives, and actions have also frozen at some point in his past. A mental and emotional hardening is disastrous.

Our world is changing rapidly in so many ways. For the sake of the gospel and for the sake of our well-being and personal growth, we need to adapt and change even when it is painful. We simply cannot afford to freeze.

If I were still employed full-time in the field of astronautics and insisted on using only a slide rule, I would not only be the object of ridicule, but I would also be out of a job. No moral value is attached to such a choice; it's simply a matter of relating to and working in the real world.

Until I was fourteen years old, my mother cooked on a stove fueled only by wood or coal. As soon as she could afford an electric range, she bought one. She welcomed the change.

In the small town of Garden City, Iowa, our telephone number was a single digit—9—and all you could do on a phone was make or receive a call, a far cry from today's ten-digit numbers and smartphones.

These are obvious changes that most of us receive with approval and appreciation. However, there are other changes that we may be more resistant to, and in areas where failure to change results in disaster—when our thinking freezes, when we refuse to grow and learn. When such prejudices rule our minds, we encounter great danger.

Freezing in Our Thinking

As we grow older, we may jokingly say, "There are two things I hate most to lose: first, my mind and second—well, I can't remember the second one."

The mind is a terrible thing to lose. Those whose loved ones have sunk into the abyss of old-age dementia know the sorrow of losing the person they love while they still live. Another tragedy occurs when we close and freeze our minds and fail to recognize the problem. We then suffer a mental hardening that has nothing to do with blood circulation.

As I grow older and continue to play handball, I find that my muscles are not as resilient as they were in my younger years. I pull and strain muscles I hardly knew I had. I lose the ability to reach for certain shots. I find my flexibility and mobility have diminished. My solution is, of necessity, to regularly stretch my muscles to improve my flexibility and to prevent injury. I also find I need potassium supplements to keep my muscles from painful cramping. I must carefully watch my nutritional intake for better energy. I'm always looking for new ways to improve my physical stamina and health—all for the joy of hitting a little blue ball around a court. This is not earth-shattering. But in a sense, it's physically and emotionally lifesaving for me.

Mentally and intellectually, the freezing process is similar. Some men refuse to listen and learn, especially in areas where they feel they have competence. They refuse to allow their ideas to be challenged. Experience and knowledge blind them to new ways of thinking. Businessmen today know that this is the death knell of their business. Being closed to new ways of thinking and doing is tantamount to closing your doors.

How many times have our children said privately, "It's no use discussing it with Dad. His mind is made up"? I suspect it has been said about me. I see that pattern in myself enough to frighten me. Is discussion with us futile because others know our opinions will never change?

How about freezing spiritually? The more we grow in knowledge and spiritual experience, the more intractable we can become, refusing to gain new insights and disciplines or to challenge some of our long-held doctrinal stands. We can become brittle and hard in our beliefs and intolerant of new believers who are growing and discovering. I'm not at all advocating abandoning your basic beliefs. But be open to other insights and experiences. This is spiritual growth.

We need to examine our patterns and habits. They're established early in life. Culture, family, friends, and education set many of our patterns and habits. By the time we reach age twenty-five, most patterns are set, altering only in minor ways in succeeding years.

How can we know if our thinking patterns are frozen? We may wish to be open-minded and teachable, yet we're uncertain about whether we project that attitude to others.

Here are some clues to assess how flexible we are in our thinking.

Analyze Your Anger toward New Ideas

Do you feel yourself getting angry at new ideas or change? When someone tries to teach you, how do you respond? Do you find yourself reacting negatively toward younger men and women who want to try new ideas, including ideas that you've tried before that didn't work for you? When that happens, watch out! Your anger is a sign of freezing.

Watch Negative and Critical Responses

Do you frequently look for the negative in a new idea? Do you excuse yourself by assuming this is a wise approach to avoid mistakes? Or could a critical spirit be a part of your personality? Negative responses often indicate a reluctance to listen and change. If negativity or criticism is frequent or increasing in your life, you may be entering a freezing stage in life. With my analytical engineering background, I find it easy to criticize and pick things apart. It's part of my training. Although it helps me in decision-making, it hinders me in hearing new ideas that I haven't helped develop.

Learn to Adapt

One of my friends, a former director of innovation at the US Air Force Academy, would say, "Adapt or die" and "Innovate or die." Both may sound extreme, but they're true. One frequently cited example is the

Kodak Corporation. Kodak didn't foresee sweeping changes—from film to digital—in the photography industry. They were late to change and declared bankruptcy in 2012.

As technological changes occur at an increasing rate, we may feel like we're far behind the curve. We suffer sensory overload. We resent our computer becoming outmoded in two years. We tire of trying to keep up with language changes, new products, new television programs. The changes seem unrelenting. We long for the familiar.

Although we tire of change, we cannot freeze the clock of progress. When we learn to accept change and adapt to it, we can make it work to our advantage as we grow in understanding. We learn to adapt. We remain fresh and vigorous in our learning processes.

If you're only in your twenties or thirties, don't be fooled by the idea that freezing won't affect you. Our habits develop early, and resistance to change can occur at any age.

Embrace the future. Embrace and evaluate what is new. Experience it. Keep what is good and discard the rest. This attitude gives evidence of a growing and vital mind.

Overcome a Lack of Curiosity

My grandson Joshua is exceptionally curious. From the time he could walk, he has been a confirmed knob-turner, switch-thrower, see-what-it-does-if-I-push-it type of child. He thoroughly investigates anything mechanical. When he enters a room, he immediately focuses on any item with moving parts or switches or handles.

Every child learns through curiosity. A child keeps learning every day—driven by curiosity. It's a shame that adults lose that childlike interest in the world about them.

I enjoy interacting with older people who keep their curiosity at a high level, who ask questions, who try new things. Rather than turning inward to worry about looks or health or reputation, they continue to learn and grow.

For many years I visited with my former high school history teacher, Louis Livingston, and his wife, Margery Livingston. Louis lived to age

107. We discussed world issues, current events, and politics. He and Margery were vitally interested in my work. Louis brought his experience to bear on current issues, and he would include only a vague recounting of the past. It was a refreshing time. He challenged my thinking, just as he had when I was a high school senior.

Don't let your curiosity freeze. Become an inveterate observer. Ask questions. Keep learning. Curiosity, observation, and learning indicate your mental flexibility and will provide new patterns of thinking.

Be an advocate of good change.

Avoid the Personality Excuse

"Can an Ethiopian change his skin or a leopard its spots?" (Jeremiah 13:23). One of my nightmares is that my children, grandchildren, or coworkers will say, "Don't bother talking to him. That's just the way he is. He's got his mind made up, and he won't change."

Sadly, that's probably true to some extent. I'm stubborn, and I know that stubbornness is no virtue. I know I have a certain kind of personality, verified by more psychological profiles and tests than I care to count. I also know how difficult it is to change the basic aspects of my personality.

From young adulthood on, our personalities—with their quirks, foibles, imperfections, and virtues—seem to harden. Too often we say, by words or actions, "This is the way I am. Accept me as I am because I can't—I won't—change."

We should hold high respect for people who continue trying to change. An acquaintance who has a reputation of being a curmudgeon and who usually only wears a T-shirt and shorts once told me, "If they're my friends, they won't care. If they're not my friends, I don't care." Such an attitude will isolate us and eventually kill our spirits. We violate a key law of mental survival—the willingness to change.

The apostle Paul makes this assessment for believers: "If anyone is in Christ, the new creation has come: The old has gone, the new is here!" (2 Corinthians 5:17). Changing and developing are firm principles of the new birth. God can change any aspect of our personalities that needs changing.

The introvert can learn to be more outgoing. The voluble and sociable can learn to guard their tongues. The critical can learn to avoid cutting and hurtful comments. The quick-tempered can learn to curb anger. We can choose to change.

We're in great danger of freezing when we think, *That's just the way I am.* We can avoid that danger by thinking, *My personality is there for God to mold, change, and use.*

Evaluate Prejudices

Prejudice exists in every part of the world. Color, race, language, looks, family background, wealth, and education all provide breeding grounds for prejudice. It's a poison that begins when we're small children, and it can destroy us as adults.

We understand prejudice intellectually. But inwardly we still fight the bigotry we may have collected from our families and communities. As we grow older, our prejudices may harden and develop in subtle ways.

Hopefully, we subdue and obliterate the more heinous biases of race, gender, and nationality. Other biases may creep in, though, and we may develop new prejudices that we try to express as "convictions." Occasionally we even appeal to the Bible, as many people did during the days of slavery.

We express some of these prejudices in our views of music, hairstyles, worship formats, clothing fashions, politics, social issues, or personal activities. What we think are convictions are really prejudices when we have no sound biblical foundations for them. Prejudice judges and condemns others. Prejudice says, "I know better. I am right."

Prejudice is often the result of our upbringings and our early environments, when we formed ideas without foundation, opinions without reason, judgments without mercy, feelings without fact.

All of us carry prejudice, both known and unrecognized. The key is to keep from freezing in these prejudices, to uproot biases that are unbiblical, and to learn to change the way we think. When we see ourselves becoming more opinionated, more critical, more inflexible in our thoughts, we're in danger of freezing in our prejudices.

Stages of Adult Development

To live, one must grow and keep on growing. It's an axiom of life. Studies have shown that when men retire, they're likely to die within a few years unless they keep interested, active, and growing. The moment we stop growing intellectually and personally, we begin dying. Sadly, this can happen at any age. We can freeze even in our youth.

The Bible's book of wisdom, Proverbs, tells us:

- Let the wise listen and add to their learning, and let the discerning get guidance. (1:5)
- If you love learning, you love the discipline that goes with it—how shortsighted to refuse correction! (12:1, MSG)
- Wise men and women are always learning, always listening for fresh insights. (18:15, MSG)

I see patterns in the decades of life. We categorize the "terrible twos" and other developmental ages for children, and we can do the same for adults:

- Our twenties—the age of learning
- Our thirties—the age of accomplishment
- Our forties—the age of relearning
- Our fifties—the age of learning and growing, or freezing and dying
- Our sixties and beyond—the age of character and influence

The Age of Learning

In our twenties, we prepare for life and work. Our attitude is one of learning, discovering, and experimenting. Life offers opportunity and hope. We seek and accept education, experience, and training as the norm. We receive correction and counsel. In many ways, our lives are blank pages waiting to be filled with our life stories. It's an exciting time of life.

I experienced an insatiable appetite for learning during my twenties when I was involved in the early days of America's space program at

Cape Canaveral. I found out how little I knew, and I hungered to grow. I sought opportunities for growth. I also saw my need to grow and change in my relationship with my family and with God. I knew I needed to change and mature. Everything was a challenge and a door to the future.

The Age of Accomplishment

In our thirties we see more clearly what we can do. We apply ourselves to our chosen tasks. We have strength, will, ambition, and drive. Although we still learn, our hunger for learning diminishes, replaced by refined abilities that directly contribute to doing our task. Life becomes intense. Children have come along or are coming along. Our marriages can fray at the edges, or even break. The life of the Spirit and of reflection recedes under the necessity of survival and the drive to accomplish. Without knowing it, our learning curve narrows to the necessary.

Questions of career, family, and purpose surface momentarily, but they usually receive only cursory attention. Many midlife issues begin to emerge. We can see the potential—or lack thereof—in our job and career. We sense the need for more attention to marriage and family. We become complacent in spiritual issues often due to the pressures of life. Without realizing it, our life foundations are being eroded.

The Age of Relearning

In our forties we find that we must "go back to school." Career fields can change drastically and even disappear. Lack of learning and development in our thirties catches up with us in our forties. Relearning, retooling, and changing careers may become necessary. We make the change, often out of necessity rather than desire. And we may get a new lease on life. At this point, the cracks in our marriages and the needs of our children become overwhelming. The famous midlife crisis hits many men with hurricane force.

In spite of the difficulties, the forties give us great opportunities for rebuilding the right foundations, growing the right roots in every area of our lives. We're attracted to helpful seminars on marriage and family, to more education and training in our work, and to reading about the how-tos of life.

Our early losses, our sin, and our pride have taken their toll. This is a teachable time of life. Relearning is a must, but it would be much easier if it were developed as a pattern earlier in life.

The Age of Learning and Growing—or of Freezing and Dying

The fifties may be the most critical time of all. During this period, a man makes a choice to either freeze or grow. Doing, learning, and growing must work together. He keeps doing his work of life out of necessity, but doing is not enough.

We live in a society where whole career fields disappear with regularity, and new ones appear with seeming spontaneity. In this information age where knowledge multiplies astronomically in only a few years, a man cannot remain stagnant and still be competitive in his work. Learning must continue. Individual growth ensures future contribution and happiness in later years.

The alternatives are frightening: freezing and beginning to die.

Although learning and growth come naturally to a few, most of us must pursue them purposefully. The cliché of "Been there, done that!" so easily characterizes our attitude. We grow tired. We want to relax. Change frustrates us more and more. We long for the old days.

But the past is only a memory. It cannot be recovered. Its lessons, however, can guide us to the future. This is a biblical pattern:

- Remember how the LORD your God led you! (Deuteronomy 8:2)
- The LORD is the one who goes ahead of you; He will be with you. He will not fail or forsake you. (Deuteronomy 31:8, NASB)
- Choose you this day whom ye will serve. (Joshua 24:15, KJV)

Growth is moving from the past to the future under God's leading. Freezing is a refusal to grow and change. The results imprison us to the past.

The Age of Character and Influence

The sixties and beyond are the age of character and influence—but only if a man continues to grow and learn. Deciding to grow and to keep growing is a sign of maturity. This involves spiritual growth that leads to spiritual maturity and personal growth that leads to personal maturity. What spiritual growth entails is clear: It involves developing depth in the Scriptures, newfound obedience to God and His Word, and a deepening of character.

Personal growth is not as clear. The secular world often understands it better than the spiritual world. Are spiritual and personal growth connected? Most certainly. Personal growth without spiritual progress is empty—as is so easily seen in how the world is ruled.

General of the Army Omar Bradley expressed well the lack of wisdom in the world: "We have grasped the mystery of the atom and rejected the Sermon on the Mount. . . . The world has achieved brilliance without wisdom, power without conscience. Ours is a world of nuclear giants and ethical infants."[1]

Spiritual growth without personal growth is an oxymoron, since true spiritual growth and maturity involve the whole person. Lack of personal and spiritual growth leaves us ineffective in influencing the world for Christ and robs us of the fullness of life that God wants us to enjoy. Personal growth is the development of our mind and emotions. It allows us to see the world around us with understanding. It connects us to those without Christ. It makes us stable and complete.

The Key to Change and Growth

The secret to true spiritual, intellectual, and emotional growth is humility. A true learner's spirit is a direct outgrowth of humility.

We first learn from Christ, just as He says: "Take my yoke upon you and learn from me" (Matthew 11:29). We need to be spiritual sponges. After knowing Christ for many decades, I find a great temptation to relax and to live off my past knowledge. After all, I've done a lot of Bible study. I've wrestled with major decisions. I've tried to think through and study many areas of spiritual life. I've come to certain conclusions.

Do I still need to study and develop? Yes, it's imperative. Who's to say I haven't made significant errors in my study?

Does God want to teach me more? Certainly.

I can easily fall into the trap of being the "answer man," always having a reply to the significant questions of spiritual life. What arrogance that would be.

One man in his forties said, "There aren't many people who can teach me much anymore." But any of us can learn from the youngest and simplest believer. Every person you meet knows something that you don't. We can learn something from everyone. The Holy Spirit gives insight to every follower of Christ. Even when I've carefully thought through issues, I can listen and learn if I'll only humble myself to do so.

I frequently need to be immersed in the Scriptures so that my spiritual life is not fed from the leftovers of the past. I need to push toward God and His Word daily in devotional time and in deeper study.

Winston Churchill once said on the floor of the British Parliament, "Personally, I am always ready to learn, although I do not always like being taught."[2] We need an openness to being taught by anyone. In our personal lives and in our careers, learning prevents stagnation and obsolescence. Keep the heat on! Don't freeze!

Freezing in Relationships

In addition to freezing in our thinking and our willingness to grow and change, we also can freeze in our relationships.

Freezing in Marriage

We often see marriage relationships reduced to a minimal necessity—functional communication, a moderate amount of argument, some level of tension, obligatory sexual activity, and public togetherness. Love is still there and commitment remains strong, yet something has left the relationship. We stop growing. In fact, we regress.

Mary and I have seen that tendency several times in our marriage. When the children were young, it seemed that we lived in separate worlds, meeting at the point of crisis or necessary decisions. I was intent on work, career, and spiritual outreach. She was intent on child-rearing and supporting our complex social and spiritual outreach lifestyle. We sensed stagnation in our relationship. Recognition of this—and some conflict—helped us work through it to keep growing.

But the problem repeats itself. It's like growing a garden. It takes constant attention, or it dies or becomes choked with weeds. Mary and I have found that we regularly—at least yearly—need to assess where we are in our life and relationship. We've found that we must reaffirm our activities and personal direction. We've tried to take time apart together just to talk and rebuild our relationship.

The danger occurs when a couple allows the stagnation to settle in and become the norm. What's the danger? It's far more than a simple dulling of the relationship. If not heeded, it can lead to divorce, or at least a disastrous pattern for our children to observe and imitate.

Freezing in Other Relationships

Other relationships can also be damaged. We easily fall into lifeless patterns with our children, relatives, and close friends. You can imagine the conversation that our relationships are reduced to. How's the weather? How are the kids? What's been happening? How were the holidays? Then . . . silence. Well, we'll talk later.

Does that sound familiar? It does to me. I've done it many times. In some relationships, that kind of conversation is sufficient. But if that's the pattern with important relationships with children or good friends, freezing is already happening.

The remedy cannot be abrupt or instantaneous. Simply begin to go beyond the routine and mundane. Give others extra time and attention. Open yourself up a little. Share more of what's going on inside you. Work at transforming your relationships with your children according to their ages. If they're now adults, move to a more adult friendship, not just a parental relationship that got stuck in the strained communication of their teens.

One last thought about areas that freeze: Some of us may be stuck in patterns of sin. If you recognize these patterns in your life, I encourage you to go back and review the discussion in part 2 of this book. One of the central reasons for freezing in our minds and relationships is becoming bogged down by persistent sin in our lives. When that happens, we certainly find it difficult to grow and develop in other areas of our lives.

Thawing Out from the Freeze

Several times in my life, I've been outside in bitterly cold weather. Almost without knowing it, my fingers, toes, face, and ears were numb with near frostbite. When I came back to the warmth of my house, my body began to thaw. As it thawed, pinpricks of intense pain appeared all over. However, I knew this was temporary. I needed to endure the pain as life-giving blood flowed back into the surface of my skin.

Thawing out after freezing in an area of life is a bit like that—there's some pain in the process. But the pain is well worth the result, and it's necessary to revive the whole.

I want to encourage you that the effort you give to growing in all these areas will result in such a greater joy in life that the pain will soon be forgotten. Larry Crabb expressed it well:

> Life can be tough. And godly people will feel its impact. . . . When bad passions seem to have the upper hand, we must remind ourselves that God is working to entice us with the prospect of knowing him, and he is appealing to parts of our souls that are not drawn to lesser pleasures. And these parts define who we really are as Christians.
>
> God's method of drawing us closer to him is to disrupt the fallen structure by allowing us to feel the terror and pain the structure was designed to overcome. He then entices us with the hope of finding in him the satisfaction of every noble desire.[3]

That hope and satisfaction he describes is indeed something we'll find as we step into the unfrozen future.

16

THE DANGER
OF CONFUSION

I WAS DRIVING ALONE AT NIGHT in Birmingham, England, before the days of GPS. I was lost. Perhaps not really lost, since I had some idea where I was. But I recognized none of the street names, and I couldn't tell if I was going toward or away from my destination.

I started down one street. After a mile, I knew it was wrong. I went back to where I started and tried another route. I realized I was thoroughly confused. While I was trying to remember to drive on the left, to give way on the roundabouts, and generally to not do something stupid, I *felt* stupid. I knew I was close, but I was disoriented. After further trial and error, I finally arrived at my destination.

When I drive in a strange city, I know I'll eventually figure out the right route, but the process of wrong turns, misjudgments, and confusing streets becomes frustrating. I soon forget the new sights around me and become totally absorbed in finding my way.

Life is like that, often at the most inconvenient of times. One of the most disconcerting feelings a man can have is confusion. Men want to know where they're going and how to get there without asking for directions. Uncertainty troubles us. We want to be responsible and directed.

All men will face confusion, probably at several points in their lives. Like many other dangers described earlier, confusion sneaks up and catches us unaware. We're traveling comfortably down a pathway and suddenly find the way obscured. It's as if we're in a fog. We can't see clearly. Our thinking processes get muddled. Our ability to make decisions seems blocked. We aren't just lost looking for the right road; we may not even know where we want to go.

This confusion can result in divorce, escape into alcohol, a revived adolescence, depressing career changes, loss of motivation, or spiritual rebellion.

If you've been through this kind of confusion, or you're experiencing it now, you recognize immediately what I'm saying. If you haven't experienced it, you're probably thinking, *That won't happen to me.* But it will.

When it happens at a certain age, we may call this confusion a "midlife crisis." But it's more than that. It can occur at any time, at any age. And it's dangerous.

Journalist Gail Sheehy called this "middlescence," which she defined as "adolescence the second time around. Turning backward, going around in circles, feeling lost in a buzz of confusion and unable to make decisions."[1]

Growth and Change Breed Confusion

Men—and women too—face confusion at several points in their lives.

In our teens, the vexing questions are: *Who do I want to become? What do I want to do? What kind of character do I want? I've got to stop playing and start working, but working at what?*

In young adulthood and early marriage, the questions are these: *How can I balance the demands of wife, children, and career? Have I chosen the right career? I'm not sure I like my work all that much.*

In the middle years, we're thinking these things: *How can I handle this crisis with our teenagers? What about my job disappointment, my job loss, my strained marriage? I'm troubled by my decreasing physical prowess.*

And in our fifties: *Why do I have so many physical problems? How can I handle this dead-end career and all the financial pressures? I'm fearful of retirement and the empty nest. My marital stress is heavy.*

In his discussion of the stages of manhood, Robert Hicks writes,

> Others may struggle more with the confusion that confronting
> their own mortality can bring. Still others may have difficulty
> accepting the fact that many of their unfulfilled yearnings will
> never be satisfied.

He adds this:

> Confusion is normative for the masculine journey as you move
> from one stage to another. Don't let the confusion be a problem
> for you. This is transition time, and transitions always breed
> confusion.[2]

Confusion is a normal experience, fraught with many dangers and
detours. The clarity and direction that come into focus as we emerge
from confusing periods of life are well worth the trip.

Earlier I spoke of inevitable losses. These losses cause us to think
differently, or to stop thinking logically. We either directly or vaguely
entertain questions like these:

- *Who am I?*
- *Why am I in this marriage?*
- *Why didn't I get promoted?*
- *Why haven't I realized my dreams?*
- *What will I do if this new thing doesn't work out?*
- *Why did I get divorced?*
- *Do my children love and respect me?*
- *Why was I unfaithful?*
- *Why am I dependent on alcohol?*
- *Why am I not happy now that I've achieved my goals?*

In wrestling with these questions, we become vulnerable, unstable, per-
plexed. Yes, confused.

Along with the confusion that we all can face through major life issues and circumstances—family, finances, health, and death—we can experience confusion in relation to our calling and vocation. These two speeding trains—calling and major life issues—often seem to hit us at once. Let's dig a bit more into the notion of calling, with its human and spiritual components and how we can navigate the confusion that our calling can bring.

Calling and Vocation

Work is life for most men. Our identity is deeply intertwined with our work. We would deny the adage "I am what I do," yet so much of a man's existence is consumed by work. His livelihood depends on work. His self-image focuses largely on how his work is progressing.

Calling and Career

Certainly, a man who is married cares about his wife and children. But to support them he needs to work. He has other drives—sports, hobbies, relationships, and travel—but work dominates. In the early stages of a man's life, his job and career capture most of his thoughts.

Inevitably, this centeredness on work is invaded by confusion. Job satisfaction starts to fray. Most jobs lose their luster as one settles into routine and reality. We become unsettled, looking for a new challenge, higher pay, a better company, or some element of enjoyment in work that has eluded us in our current job.

Some men stay in a less-than-satisfying job simply because they must. Tenure, education, age, or finances prohibit a job change. Then image and identity begin to crack. The engineer thinks he really wants to be an artist. The construction worker finds he wants a college degree. The teacher tires of children and wants to be in business. The lack of satisfaction brings us to confusion and decision. The risk of change is great, so many men choose to live in the confusion, unwilling to move to a new focus.

A job change can lead to confusion or new encouragement. Often a job change is forced upon us. The company transfers us. Our position disappears. We move for the sake of our family. When such a change is strictly of our own choosing, we do well. But confusion and disorientation often develop when external circumstances force us to change.

Joseph, the son of Jacob, had a number of huge changes thrust upon him (the full story is in Genesis 37–50). He went from being his father's favorite son in a position of privilege to being a slave in Egypt. Then, after he had worked his way to the top of Potiphar's household staff, he was falsely accused and thrown into prison. Talk about confusion! Yet he always set about to make the best of his circumstances.[3]

I've known men who had to take a lesser job than they wanted and were trained for. Some spent years in discouragement or confusion. Others set out to make the best of it, sensing God's hand in their circumstances.

Having a job that's in jeopardy is even more confusing. Downsizing, performance reviews, and competition can put our jobs in danger. Many men are living month by month, not knowing if they'll have a job. Men in seasonal or project work face threats of cancellation. The tension of uncertainty and vulnerability leads to the stress of confusion. Our egos and sense of value get damaged. We feel like a piece of property in the job market.

This is the confusion:

- *Am I valuable?*
- *Am I expendable?*
- *Am I competent enough to be wanted?*

When a job seems secure, then the drive for job success takes over. But success is such a relative concept. It's measured largely by our past and our peers.

Since I travel frequently in poor countries, I see that for many men, just having employment and getting paid is success. But for most of us in the Western world, we see success as increasing pay scales and promotions. Our expectations of ourselves drive us.

Unfortunately, we'll max out. At some point—early or later in life—we'll view ourselves as having failed. At that point, we become confused. *Did I pick the wrong career? What if I'd done this or that—would I have been more successful?*

There's another side to the pursuit of success. Some men who are quite successful will discover it to be an empty achievement, particularly if they achieve it at the expense of their families or their spiritual lives. Then they enter a time of regret and confusion. *Was it worth it? What did it cost me? Is this all there is to it?*

The Other Calling

For the lay believer, *calling* has usually meant "vocation." The other calling that many recognize is the calling to spiritual or religious service. This division does great disservice to the layman. This is not to disparage a calling to vocational ministry but to clarify that it's not the only spiritual calling.

Every believer in Christ has, or should have, a spiritual calling. We each have gifts and talents from God that He wants us to use to the maximum. Most men use their gifts and talents in the secular marketplace.

In the spiritual realm, men usually engage in a grab-bag approach to their efforts, giving themselves to whatever is needed, available, or requested. This results in most men functioning outside their spiritual gifts. It also leads to doing too many things. Of course, some men do nothing in the spiritual realm, resulting in great poverty of spirit. This lack of focus leads to discouragement and confusion, not only in spiritual endeavors but in life in general.

Every Christian—not just the pastor or vocational Christian worker—is spiritually called. But most men haven't clarified that calling or acted on it. Only when a man's spiritual calling and vocational calling are in balance will his confusion begin to disappear.

The Keys to Conquering Confusion

Gail Sheehy describes the fifties for men as "the Flaming Fifties" or "flameout."[4] I've seen both. Some men at this stage thrive, while others thrash about, never coming to a sense of direction for their lives.

Sheehy describes men at this passage as "in disillusionment about themselves or having adjusted their aspirations downward."[5] What do men worry about? Losing their hair and a decreasing ability in sports!

Sheehy points out that men who see themselves on the downside of a career "become frustrated and depressed and feel worthless, *no matter what they have achieved up to that point.*"[6]

This leads us to consider two keys to overcoming or avoiding confusion.

Surrender

No one likes to give up. There's something in the male ego that hates quitting. We want to conquer, to succeed. When a person surrenders in human terms, such as to the law, it means giving up the freedom to do as you wish and to follow the will of another. We do this regularly in marriage—a husband surrenders what he wants to the needs and wishes of his wife. We also do it at work, obeying the directions of an employer.

In the life of a believer in Christ, surrender means turning your life unreservedly and irrevocably over to Him. That's what Jesus means when He says, "If anyone wishes to come after Me, he must deny himself, and take up his cross daily and follow Me" (Luke 9:23, NASB). I like the phrasing in *The Message*: "Anyone who intends to come with me has to let me lead. You're not in the driver's seat—I am. Don't run from suffering; embrace it. Follow me and I'll show you how."

Jesus once brought up the Old Testament story of Lot's wife, who disobeyed God and looked back on her cherished life in Sodom then immediately turned into a pillar of salt. Jesus said, "Remember what happened to Lot's wife! If you grasp and cling to life on your terms, you'll lose it, but if you let that life go, you'll get life on God's terms" (Luke 17:32-33, MSG).

"Let that life go." This is surrender. It's having life on God's terms. He wants us to surrender to His sovereignty in all our circumstances, even in our confusion. This is surrender to

- where God put me,
- who I am,
- my past,
- my gifts,

- my suffering,
- my disappointments,
- my illnesses,
- my losses.

The way through the fog of confusion is to surrender your will to God for anything He wants you to do. This means submitting to God's authority and plan for your life.

Many times in my life, I wasn't really pleased with the plans God had obviously brought my way. When our thirty-year-old son was murdered, I entered a period of confusion. *What is God doing? Why? Why Steve?* The haze of the succeeding months was too thick, seemingly impenetrable. I thought I would never emerge from the grief and confusion.

Only as I began to submit and surrender to God in these terrible circumstances did peace and focus return. In fact, the focus of my life became much clearer. I realized that many of my previous motivations were tainted with pride and ego.

I remember other times when my job wasn't going as well as I expected. I struggled with what I should do about criticism and conflicting counsel regarding my leadership in The Navigators. I was urged to lead with stronger authority, but I had no peace (or was it courage?) to do that. I chose to wait—a difficult thing for me, since I'm a doer. There were periods of confusion as to whether I was doing the right thing. It took a couple of years to confirm the direction I felt God had led me. Gradually the confusion cleared, and I was confident of God's direction. But I had to surrender myself, my reputation, and my own tendencies.

It's always easier to look back on the struggles of confusion with twenty-twenty hindsight. But in the midst of these events, life wasn't so clear.

If you're in a period of confusion, I urge you to surrender to God . . . and then *wait*. Wait for Him to clarify your direction. Don't act hastily on a job change, a divorce, a lawsuit, a move, or a large financial commitment. Let the confusion dissipate. And then, when God makes the timing clear, *act*.

The LORD longs to be gracious to you;
     therefore he will rise up to show you compassion.
For the LORD is a God of justice.
     Blessed are all who wait for him!
ISAIAH 30:18

Job struggled in his confusion and argued with God about his condition. His friend Elihu, though limited in his understanding of God's ways, seemingly spoke correctly when he said, "It is even more false to say that he doesn't see what is going on. He *does* bring about justice at last if you will only wait" (Job 35:14, TLB).

Like surrender, waiting is difficult. It's one of the most significant expressions of faith. We ask our children to wait for dessert, or wait for Christmas, or wait for the weekend. They do wait, partly because they have no choice but also because they trust us to be true to our promise of what will come after the waiting.

Likewise, God will be true to His word as we wait.

Oswald Chambers, my favorite devotional author, speaks often of both surrender and waiting, as in these words:

> There is only one thing God wants of us, and that is our
> unconditional surrender. . . . Have we come to the place where
> God can withdraw His blessings and it does not affect our trust
> in Him? When once we see God at work, we will never bother
> our heads about things that happen, because we are actually
> trusting in our Father in heaven Whom the world cannot see.
>
> Wait on God and He will work, but don't wait in spiritual
> sulks because you cannot see an inch in front of you! Are we
> detached enough from our own spiritual hysterics to wait on
> God? To wait is not to sit with folded hands, but to learn to do
> what we are told.[7]

So we surrender and wait. . . .

Clarify Your Life Message

In addition to surrendering to God and waiting for Him, there's another avenue He wants us to pursue to clear up our confusion.

When we're young, we generally pursue a number of interests, trying to find out what we do well and what we enjoy. As we go on in life, we discover our abilities and talents and try to focus on using them. We're privileged to live in a country where it's fairly easy to change jobs and even careers. But much frustration in work results from the failure to match our jobs with our talents and abilities.

Our work is not who we are, however, in spite of being pigeonholed by the kind of job we have. What do we really want to be known for? Being a good father? A faithful husband? A man of integrity? A generous man? A lover of God? A citizen with the correct political views?

In short: *What is my life message? What is my life mission?*

A life message is the combination of your spiritual and vocational callings. It could be answered by responding to these questions: *What drives me? What am I motivated to do?*

When you think of a famous person, you automatically consider his or her life message. For Billy Graham, it was evangelism. For Mother Teresa, it was compassion for the helpless. For John D. Rockefeller, it was money and business. For Muhammad Ali, it was being the greatest boxer. You can think of many others whose messages include money, power, a beautiful house, success, winning, or being the best at something. Others have no message at all. They seem to have no distinguishing drive to their lives.

I love to play handball. But that's not what I want to be known for. (Little chance of that, considering my level of play!) I held rank in the Air Force Reserve, but I don't want to be remembered primarily as a general. In terms of real life meaning, that would be quite empty.

A life message is something that God brings out in our lives as we grow spiritually. All other areas of our lives—our jobs, homes, lifestyles, accomplishments—become a vehicle for that message.

The apostle Paul once said, "This one thing I do" (Philippians 3:13,

KJV), or as *The Living Bible* expresses it, "I am bringing all my energies to bear on this one thing." Paul then said, "I press toward the mark for the prize of the high calling of God in Christ Jesus" (3:14, KJV). Paul knew where he was going and why he was going there. The passion of Paul's life was to serve God and to bring the gospel of Christ to the world.

To be meaningful, our life message needs to be rooted in God and His call to us. Everything else is secondary. This doesn't at all imply that we must have a full-time Christian vocation. *It does mean being driven by what is on God's heart for us.*

Knowing our life message or life direction is key to bringing order out of our confusion. Here's another way to phrase the overarching question: *What is my primary ministry and purpose?*

For some people, it's helpful to develop a personal mission statement, much as we would do for a company, department, or church. After many years, it has become quite clear to me that I'm driven by two purposes. The first is relating to people from each of the different environments of my life who don't know Christ personally, trying to communicate the gospel to them. The second is seeing believers grow to a point where they reproduce their lives spiritually, reaching and discipling others.

This has been a passion for me not only in my time working with The Navigators but also beyond that; I didn't adopt this driving purpose just to get a job. I came to the job because this was my life message.

I've occasionally been asked to be a candidate to lead other organizations. Those who tried to recruit me found it difficult to see that I was driven more by my life message than by a job responsibility.

Other purposes I've observed include prayer, evangelism, integrity in business, missions, caring for the helpless, reaching children and young teens, helping a church body develop, and teaching.

Here are some questions to help you develop your life message:

1. *Am I a believer in Christ?* (If not, there can be no totally satisfying life message.)
2. *Am I trying to follow Christ with all my heart, soul, and mind?* (This provides the soil in which a life message grows.)

3. *What are my human talents and spiritual gifts?*
4. *What have I enjoyed doing?*
5. *What have I done well?*
6. *What have I seen God bless in my life?*
7. *In the spiritual realm, what drives me?*
8. *What opportunities do I have to serve?*
9. *How does my work fit in my life?*
10. *What do my wife and friends think drives me?*
11. *What has God been saying to me through His Word?*

Overcoming Confusion

Sometimes our confusion is from God, as He uses it in order to direct us toward discovering what He wants us to do. Let's not miss what He's saying to us.

Confusion reigns when we become disoriented. Disorientation has been the cause of tragic crashes of ships and airplanes. Every pilot or ship captain could tell story after story of near collisions due to not knowing their precise position or altitude. In March of 1977, two 747s were taxiing in opposite directions on the same runway in dense fog at an airport in the Canary Islands, unable to see each other and having unclear radio communications with the control tower. One plane accelerated to take off. The resulting collision and explosive fires resulted in 583 deaths.

In life, knowing where we are and where we're going erases confusion and disorientation. Knowing our calling and life message aids us in times of confusion.

Simply recognizing the possibility of such confusion is a great help in overriding the resulting danger. When confusion strikes, take time to seek God, to understand more of His will for you—and to get your direction straight.

17

THE DANGER
OF WITHDRAWAL

IN THE MIDST OF CONFUSION, many men choose to withdraw—from family, from friends, from spiritual endeavors—and to put up a protective wall around themselves.

A business executive was struggling to make friends because his company moved him so frequently. He'd experienced good friendships but found it difficult to leave them when he moved. He said, "I finally solved the problem. I don't make friends anymore."

Another man began having difficulty at work while experiencing marriage strain at home. He began to withdraw from his friends, embarrassed at his perceived failures. He didn't want to discuss them or receive advice. When he first brought up the issues to some close friends, their responses were not helpful. They either rebuked him or ignored him. Trying to reach out left him discouraged, so he gradually withdrew.

Other men come to a point in their lives when something snaps spiritually. Once they were faithful to God, seemingly committed and spiritually active; later they began to doubt and to allow their spiritual disciplines to decrease. They gave in to small sins. Finally, slowly, they withdrew from God. While this withdrawal was developing, they might never have known the exact cause or even perceived what they were doing. But the result was a cooled fervor for God and a consequent eroding of faith.

In each of these vignettes, the precipitating event could have involved loss, sin, stagnation, or confusion. The result is the same—withdrawal from people who can help and withdrawal from God.

Withdrawal rarely results from a conscious decision. More often it follows a series of small steps in a wrong direction.

Withdrawal from God

"Because of the increase of wickedness, the love of most will grow cold" (Matthew 24:12). This is a frightening verse. It's like being told on your wedding day that in two years' time you'll have stopped loving your wife and will file for divorce. Impossible! Never! After all, you've just pledged to love "till death do us part."

The context of Jesus' statement was the end times of tribulation, war, persecution, and false prophets. It makes me wonder: *Will my own love for God grow cold?* I think not, yet I've seen enough signs in my spiritual life to tell me the possibility exists. Some of those signs include mechanical responses in my relationship with Him, a loss of fervor for Him, and spiritual dryness.

The spiritual life can easily become a series of mechanical acts of service and activities. Attending church becomes a ritual, an obligation instead of an act of worship and fellowship. Daily Bible reading slips to a few times during the week, becoming perfunctory and rigid. Bible study becomes a chore. Prayer is lifeless, lacking any real connection with God.

In her book *Enjoying the Presence of God*, Jan Johnson reflects:

I remember the day my quiet time died. After gathering all my devotional props, I settled into a terrible emptiness. I needed God as I had never needed Him before, but my regimented prayers were puny containers for my anguish.[1]

Israel's Withdrawal

Speaking through the prophet Isaiah, God told the nation of Israel that he was sick of their trite, meaningless sacrifices:

> I am sick of your sacrifices. Don't bring me any more of them.
> . . . Your holy celebrations of the new moon and the Sabbath, and your special days for fasting—even your most pious meetings—all are frauds! I want nothing more to do with them. . . .
>
> Quit your evil ways. Learn to do good, to be fair, and to help the poor, the fatherless, and widows. . . .
>
> If you will only let me help you, if you will only obey, then I will make you rich!
>
> ISAIAH 1:11-13, 16-17, 19, TLB

At this time, the people of Israel lived in great prosperity. But while they carried on forms of worship, their lives were sinful. They became so comfortable in their prosperity that their devotion to God eroded.

This can happen to any of us. While we do our acts of devotion, we may have lost the substance of obedience—a heartfelt worship of God and fervor for Him.

Loss of fervor for God accompanies this "going through the motions" type of relationship with Him. Fervor for God is a hunger and desire for Him. Hunger for food causes us to meet a physical, human need. Hunger is necessary; desire for food should drive us to satisfy our bodies' needs in the best way possible, not simply to quench our appetites. A desire for food affects every aspect of the food—its type, appearance, taste, and quality.

In much the same way, we want our hunger for God to meet a desperate need for spiritual well-being. We want fervor to preserve the very best in our relationship with Him. We want the desire to experience all that can be experienced with God.

David described this hunger: "You, God, are my God, earnestly I seek you; I thirst for you, my whole being longs for you, in a dry and parched land where there is no water" (Psalm 63:1). This psalm was written when David was in trouble, in all likelihood when his son Absalom betrayed him and stole the throne. David knew that all he had left was God. David was desperate enough—hungry enough—to seek God.

A similar notion is found in Psalm 42: "As the deer pants for streams of water, so my soul pants for you, my God. My soul thirsts for God, for the living God. When can I go and meet with God?" (42:1-2).

To keep our fervor alive, we need to actively seek God. Even when times are good, we can become complacent and walk away. We need to thirst for Him, knowing that only He can satisfy us. It's too easy to withdraw and try to satisfy ourselves or solve our problems alone.

Biblical Antidotes to Withdrawal

Periodically, we may go through a time of spiritual dryness when our relationship with God becomes mechanical and lackluster. What can we do before the withdrawal becomes dangerous?

I've found several steps to take that help me in a dry time.

1. *Examine your heart.* See if you're harboring known sin. If so, confess it and repent. Sin is the enemy of our relationship and fellowship with God. Hidden or secret sin is especially damaging, since we know it's there but choose to do nothing about it.

2. *Deal with unresolved conflict.* Is there an unresolved conflict you've been unwilling to face? Begin a process of facing it, and initiate reconciliation. When our lives are not right with people, they tend to not be right with God.

Having cleared the air in these two areas, here are additional ideas to try:

3. *Take a spiritual retreat.* Get away by yourself for a weekend. Get good rest. Take only your Bible and a few select books that spiritually encourage you. If a weekend isn't possible, try a couple of successive Saturday mornings.

4. *Try spiritual reading.* If you find it difficult to read extensive portions of Scripture, read or reread small portions of Scripture along with favorite devotional books such as *Words to Winners of Souls* by Horatius Bonar, *The Pursuit of God* by A. W. Tozer, *Spiritual Maturity* by J. Oswald Sanders, or *My Utmost for His Highest* by Oswald Chambers. Portions from these classics encourage my soul to hunger for God.

5. *Praise God.* Listen to praise music and sing along. Let your heart and emotions enter into your time of worship.

6. *Seek good teaching.* Attend a conference that will encourage and challenge you. How often do we get away and spend an entire weekend focused on spiritual matters?[2]

7. *Try spiritual journaling.* Journal some of your thoughts and reflections. (If you haven't journaled before, an excellent resource is *Spiritual Journaling* by Richard Peace.)[3]

8. *Try new approaches to prayer.* Spend extended time praying through some of the Psalms. Pray with a friend or a small group. Pray especially for other people and their needs. Keep a record of your prayers and their answers.

9. *Take care of your "temple"—your body.* Increase your disciplines in the areas of exercise, sleep, and diet. Being tired or physically unfit makes all of life more difficult.

10. *Seek intimate fellowship.* Spend time with another man or a small group with whom you can discuss your dryness of soul. Sometimes just talking about it will be a help.

11. *Be innovative in your devotions.* Try new approaches in your devotional time with God. Change the time, location, or format of your quiet time. If you don't have a regular time of reading the Bible and praying, start immediately.

Finally, remember that only God can bring you out of a spiritually dry period. These activities can set the stage for Him to refresh your hunger and thirst for Him. Be patient as you work at drawing near to God rather than withdrawing from Him. It's a gradual process, seldom a sudden renewal.

Withdrawal from Relationships

The next most dangerous act is to withdraw from the important relationships in your life. Most men hesitate to get close emotionally or relationally. This attitude makes it easy to draw back when you enter difficult periods of life. Men find it simple to step into emotional isolation while at the same time continuing to function at work and even in social and spiritual activities.

Withdrawal from your family produces the greatest impact on others. Your wife will see it first. She'll notice your communication closing down—even more than is normal for male communication. When you sense this happening, take it as the first sign of danger. You need your wife to walk through this time with you.

When you withdraw from your children, there's little they can do. They need you. They don't understand that you have needs, feelings, and problems. Even when you feel like distancing yourself, don't.

The easiest withdrawal is from friendships with other men. You just stop taking the initiative or responding to friends' requests for time. Have you noticed yourself giving the following excuses?

- "I've got a lot going on at work."
- "I need some extra time with the family."
- "Things have really been hectic this summer. How about trying me again in a couple of months?"

These excuses will soon lead to a complete withdrawal from talking with friends, unless they sense something's wrong and therefore pursue you all the more.

Men tend to have few intimate friends. Most of their friendships are shallow and centered on activities—goals, work, sports, and hobbies. In general, men tend to be guarded and protective in their relationships with other men. They want to share deeply but find it difficult.

This is a dangerous time because a man can easily find himself opening up emotionally to a woman other than his wife. This is frequently the genesis of extramarital affairs—needing someone to talk to, then finding someone who'll listen.

Withdrawing from friendships with other believing men closes doors to desperately needed relationships and opens doors to wrong relationships. This is a time for real accountability. It's also a time to work more diligently on building and protecting friendships with a few men.

The Role of Mentors

My life has been marked by several mentors. As I reflected on this topic of withdrawal—the idea of simply quitting in terms of putting in the effort required to live life in Christ—I thought of two of those mentors.

My earliest mentors were Bob Shepler and Bud Ponten. Bob and Bud were an unlikely pair to impact my life, but they did, very deeply. Both had many reasons to quit in life, to blame God for their difficult circumstances and simply withdraw into their own worlds. But they didn't. Instead, they reached out and influenced me and many other young men.

Bud and Bob and a few other businessmen began a Sunday school in our post–World War II neighborhood where there was no church. Both men taught my Sunday school class at one time or another. But our interaction wasn't limited merely to class.

Bob Shepler was afflicted with rheumatic fever when he was a teenager. It took him six years to complete high school. That did not keep him from taking a wild bunch of young boys to the mountains for camping, fishing, swimming—all strenuous activities that boys like to do. He was always a hard worker and a demanding businessman. I worked for Bob while I was in high school, and he taught me about people, business, and work skills.

Through the years I saw him begin to use a cane, then one crutch, then two crutches, then a wheelchair part-time. When I saw him near the end of his life, he was fully confined to the wheelchair. But it was motorized, and he kept going at age seventy-seven. He was still active and creative. He would not quit.

It was in the context of Bob's Sunday school class that I came to Christ. He recruited college students to help him reach out to kids. One of those students was Walt Nelson (later Dr. Walter Nelson, a professor of education at California State University, Northridge). Walt prayed with me to receive Christ after one of our many outings with the class.

Bud Ponten was afflicted with cerebral palsy from birth. His face was contorted. His legs required braces, and his walk was jerky and ungainly. Writing and performing manual tasks required the utmost discipline and concentration, because his fingers and hands responded so slowly.

When Bud was a teenager, his speech could barely be understood, so he sang hymns to practice his diction. Everything he did took great effort.

Bud taught me to play tennis. He taught me to work in his print shop. He hauled me around in his station wagon to many activities. It would have been easy to withdraw from Bud or to be uncomfortable around him because of his disabilities. But I knew he really loved God, and he loved kids. He was determined to make his life count for God. It would have been easy for him to withdraw into a life of self-pity and limited relationships.

Bud remained my friend for his entire life, a life constantly filled with new difficulties. His one-man print shop finally could no longer compete against big businesses. His body started breaking down. He developed problems in his neck, back, and ankles due to his struggle to walk. In his later years, he was in constant pain.

Bud was a man of the Word and a man of character. I visited him in the hospital as he lay dying of cancer. As hospital attendants were wheeling him to the operating room for surgery, I met him in the corridor. "Jerry," he said, "I've had a wonderful life! All this pain will have been worth it if it helps my children walk with Christ!"

A *wonderful* life? I'd known Bud to have only pain and difficulty. Yet he never complained, even when he was discouraged. And I never heard him complain about his physical afflictions. He was a testimony of faithfulness in adversity.

If anyone ever had a reason to quit and withdraw, Bob and Bud did. But they kept going and kept reaching out. They had purpose and focus. I'm not naive enough to think they didn't have some significant bouts of discouragement and questioning God. But they did not withdraw. Whenever I'm tempted to quit or to withdraw, I think of them. Where would *I* be if they'd chosen to sulk and feel sorry for themselves rather than reaching out to kids?

Never Give Up

In their book *A Second Helping of Chicken Soup for the Soul* Jack Canfield and Mark Hansen record the lives of many people who could have quit but didn't. Here's a sampling:

After years of progressive hearing loss, by age 46 German composer Ludwig van Beethoven had become completely deaf. Nevertheless, he wrote his greatest music, including five symphonies, during his later years.

Wilma Rudolph was the 20th of 22 children. She was born prematurely and her survival was doubtful. When she was 4 years old, she contracted double pneumonia and scarlet fever, which left her with a paralyzed left leg. At age 9, she removed the metal leg brace she had been dependent on and began to walk without it. By 13 she had developed a rhythmic walk, which doctors said was a miracle. The same year she decided to become a runner. She entered a race and came in last. For the next few years every race she entered, she came in last. Everyone told her to quit, but she kept on running. One day she actually won a race. And then another. From then on she won every race she entered. Eventually this little girl, who was told she would never walk again, went on to win three Olympic gold medals.

"My mother taught me very early to believe I could achieve any accomplishment I wanted to. The first was to walk without braces."[4]

Louis L'Amour wrote over a hundred western novels, selling over two hundred million copies. He reportedly received 350 rejections before he made his first sale.[5]

D. H. Groberg, in his poem "The Race," describes a young boy who ran a race, falling many times, yet finishing. Here's one stanza:

And to his dad he sadly said,
"I didn't do too well."
"To me, you won," his father said.
"You rose each time you fell."[6]

Don't quit! Don't withdraw from God or friends! Never give up! Keep going! With God's help, you can!

18

THE FOURTH QUARTER

THE SPORTS WORLD LIVES for the drama of the game's final minutes, in those times when the score is close and the outcome still undecided. Sometimes there's the miracle of the last-minute come-from-behind victory, the finish that makes history. Whether it's a professional sports team or a small high school team, every spectator and coach knows the game isn't over until that final second is gone from the clock.

Every fan knows the promise and the potential disaster of the fourth quarter in American football. Every team has a fourth-quarter strategy—surprise plays, a new quarterback, or a risky call. Maybe the score is 38–36. The visiting team is in the lead, but they fail to score just after the two-minute mark. The home team takes the ball and, on a long pass, quickly advances it to almost the twenty-yard line, with only a minute to go. It should be an easy field goal, and the coach has the team run two more plays till the clock shows only ten seconds. The placekicker steps in. If he makes it, they win. If not, the other team wins. The crowd is wild. The ball is snapped, the placekicker gracefully boots it . . . but the ball is barely deflected by the upraised arm of a leaping defender, and it just misses going through the goal posts.

Then the critics start the "what if" discussions.

In real life, however, "what if" does little good. Choices have to be made, and there's no going back.

Let's picture a man's life in four quarters:

1. Before age twenty: *Getting Ready*
2. Between twenty and forty: *The Big Choices*
3. Between forty and sixty: *The Productive Years*
4. After age sixty: *The Fourth Quarter*

Most of our activity in life focuses on the first three quarters.

The confluence of parents, education, and our own efforts determine so much of our early life, getting us ready for what's to come. Secular and religious literature overwhelms us with advice on this period. It's crucial and life-forming—but not fully determinative.

In the period of big choices, the most difficult childhood and adolescent experiences can be overcome. This time of big choices will dominate and determine a man's future. Marriage, career, first jobs, children, more education, divorce—all set the direction of his adult life. Successes and failures, dreams and disappointments, and subsequent critical choices mark this critical period. At this point, spiritual choices float in and out of focus as we try to just survive, with or without a focus on God. Crucial choices set the potential for success or ruin in the future. Some make choices that destroy their lives—through alcohol, drugs, or immoral actions. Others realize the destructiveness of bad choices, and they build a different foundation.

In the productive years, most men are still frantically scrambling to build or engineer a secure future. They choose an identity that says who they are—mostly by what they do or have accomplished. The marks of their success will be evident in financial security, prestige, prosperity, and a stable marriage and family. If they're Christ-followers, they want to be viewed as spiritually mature and self-sufficient. Many have experienced life crises of some magnitude—a career switch, a marriage breakup, issues with adult children, or financial reversals. They emerge scarred but hopefully wiser. Perhaps their dreams burst with the realization of lost time and opportunity.

Then comes the fourth quarter, with a chance to buy back lost time and dwindling opportunities. Unfortunately, many men are unprepared for the surprises that await them in this final period of life.

This chapter is not about retirement or even preparing for retirement. It's not about a late-life crisis or some get-your-house-in-order effort. Rather, it's about something deep in our psyche and inner motivations—our *significance* and our *identity*.

We may easily assert that if we're spiritually mature, our significance and identity reside in Christ and God. Technically and theologically that's true. But believing this truth and experiencing the reality of it can elude us and catch us by surprise. Being a follower of Jesus doesn't shield us from the emotional surprises awaiting us in the fourth quarter.

Four kinds of men will likely read this book:

1. The man who hasn't yet committed his life to Christ—a person still on a search
2. A relatively new follower of Jesus who's still learning the implications of a new life as a believer
3. A long-term follower of Christ who hasn't given much attention to spiritual growth and spiritual depth but is hungry to do so now
4. A mature believer who knows Scripture well and who has made significant commitments to God's lordship in his life

All these men will face similar issues, but they'll each possess a different foundation or background for addressing those issues.

I wish I could say that the mature believer has a broader set of tools to deal with the fourth quarter. But in many ways, depth of knowledge can give us a false sense of security. We think we won't experience the pitfalls of the fourth quarter. Although spiritual depth helps us navigate all areas of life with a deeper perspective and biblical tools, the Bible is not some magic tool for every life issue. Every circumstance needs a range of tools.

For instance, even men deeply committed to Christ experience depression, anxiety, disappointment, suffering, and yes, loss. When we're forewarned and made aware of this, we can better apply all the tools we have available to us.

Wherever you are in your spiritual journey, the fourth quarter will surprise you in many ways. This chapter will arm you with information, awareness, and perspectives for applying all the tools at your disposal. My good friend Navy Captain Terry Pierce greatly helped me identify and clarify these issues. Both of us have seen men of power, prestige, and position marry themselves to their past identities and achievements, sadly unaware of the danger this posed. With Terry's permission, here are some of his comments from our conversation:

> I was privileged to be the sole speechwriter for the chief of naval operations for two years. During this time, I wrote several change-of-command speeches for senior naval officers as well as eulogy speeches for deceased senior naval officers. It struck me that in writing the eulogy speeches, I focused on an officer's virtue and character. I rarely mentioned their "résumé virtues," such as where they went to college, their highest degrees, their various commands and accomplishments. Instead, the eulogy speech focused on what type of man this person was.
>
> The easiest speeches to write were for those naval officers who'd adopted a new fourth-quarter game plan that focused on giving back to society. The hardest speeches to write were for those officers who hadn't adopted a new game plan for the fourth quarter and whose identity was grounded in their résumé achievements accumulated in the first three quarters of life.
>
> As I began my own fourth quarter of life, I adopted a new game plan centered on the Holy Spirit. No longer was I focused on padding my résumé virtues. Who cares? No one's going to mention them at my eulogy. Instead, I started focusing on understanding the ministry of the Holy Spirit and becoming a spiritual Christian. Put simply, my fourth-quarter

game plan was accomplishing deeds by the work of the indwelling Holy Spirit.

One of my senior mentors who adopted a new fourth-quarter game plan was Gary Booth, now in his early eighties. Gary was the European vice president of research for Procter & Gamble. He has a PhD in organic chemistry and was a disruptor innovator during his career. When he retired, he focused on funding and mentoring underserved students, creating demonstration projects for alternative energy, and mentoring university professors in turning their research into new companies. In the past twenty years, he and his wife have funded over two hundred students, and many of those have gone on to receive advanced degrees and are now mentoring their own students. His six solar farms are heavily instrumented and are designed to allow students to understand the advantages and disadvantages of solar energy and how solar energy can be stored. His current focus is on harnessing the deep cold of outer space to cool structures.

When I first met this mentor, he was in the fourth quarter of his life. I could have never guessed, however, that he'd once held such a senior position in a large company. He never discussed his résumé virtues. His focus was entirely on mentoring, alternative energy, and the economic development of Appalachian poverty pockets.

In this conversation, Terry introduced me to the difference between "résumé virtues" and "eulogy virtues." Résumé virtues are ones that you use to get a job or to puff yourself up. Eulogy virtues are the character virtues that define who you really are and what's underneath all the accomplishments.

In the fourth quarter, it's time to concentrate on your eulogy virtues.

I remember so clearly an incident on a flight to Hawaii. A man was going up and down the aisle introducing himself and saying that he was a star football player in the NFL. I felt sorry for him—that this was his identity.

But how many times have I been engaged with a group of people and wanted to blurt out, "Hey, do you know who I am and what I've done?" I'm embarrassed even at the thought—and, unfortunately, it's true. I'm not so different from that football player.

The key is how we handle those kinds of thoughts and temptations—and understanding how they handle us.

Critical Losses and Issues in the Fourth Quarter

Now, let's address some specifics.

Loss of identity is a particular danger in the fourth quarter. We all have an identity, real or imagined. For some, it's an identity of achievement and accomplishment. Sometimes that identity is one of significant accomplishments or positions.

I was recently with a group of military veterans. These were ordinary men, not superstars that anyone would recognize. Almost all of them introduced themselves with some event or place—the Normandy beachhead, the name of the Navy ship they were on, the Vietnam War, the unit they served with, the battles fought and survived. Some shared what they did after their military service. They were proud of their service and their branch of service but especially thankful for their survival. One man, a ninety-seven-year-old Jewish World War II veteran, told me, "I thank God every day for protecting me." Frankly, I was impressed. These men were grateful, not prideful. I was proud to know them and honor them.

Yet each one of them is much more than just a veteran. They're all human beings with a present and future life. We never want to forget our past, but we must not let it define us. Our identity must be *who we are*, not what we were.

First, we need a reminder of how those events in our past happened.

- *Our family and background.* We did not choose our parents, our place of birth, our family, or our economic advantages or disadvantages. God ordained those things. My history of being from a small farm community in Iowa and having a Norwegian heritage, a divorced mother, and a loving grandfather—those things were not of my making.

- *Our health.* Our physical health is the result of our DNA and—to some extent—of how we've cared for ourselves. At some point, our health will fail. When we remain healthy while others become ill, we must not be proud but thankful. Our physical and mental capacities are gifts from God. The brilliant person should be grateful for the mind God gave him. Our athletic or physical ability and our level of energy—these things are also from God.

- *Our position and opportunities.* These things are rarely of our own doing. Who created your circumstances and opportunities? Who put you in the right place at the right time? Who caused you to be noticed by others in authority? In my own career, I can point to what I call "unexpected miracles of opportunity." I did nothing to make them happen; I only had to respond to them.

- *Our motivation.* Where does motivation come from? Why are we motivated to do some things and not others? All the how-to and self-help books can never explain the inner workings of our lives, things that only God can touch.

We are not self-made men. We're ordinary men responding to God's opportunities—or not. We take our God-created human selves and simply respond to the opportunities we encounter. We work hard, we plan and scheme to accomplish things and get ahead, but even then, we're using the abilities God has given us.

There are some who don't want to admit that there's a God who does these things. But it's quite a stretch of imagination to ascribe them merely to complex statistics of chance. Some*one* made us the way we are. We simply take who we are and work with the raw material of our lives.

The result of these realizations is that we're deeply and profoundly humbled. "Let the one who boasts boast in the Lord" (2 Corinthians 10:17).

At this point you may protest: "But didn't I have something to do with my success? Look at the hard work, the eighty-hour work weeks, the risks I took." All that is true and should not be discredited. But recognize who gave you the ability and opportunity and desire to work hard. All of us must apply the energy and abilities God gave us. Just keep these two truths in balance—God's gifts and our responsibility.

I would be remiss not to state the great theological truth that my identity is in Jesus Christ as a child of God. The apostle Paul portrays this for us. In defending his heritage and accomplishments he says,

> If someone else thinks they have reasons to put confidence in the
> flesh, I have more: circumcised on the eighth day, of the people
> of Israel, of the tribe of Benjamin, a Hebrew of Hebrews; in
> regard to the law, a Pharisee; as for zeal, persecuting the church;
> as for righteousness based on the law, faultless.
>
> PHILIPPIANS 3:4-6

Paul had everything a Jew of his time could want. He was at the top of his game. Then—in a spectacular way—he met Jesus and became a believer. He goes on to describe his newfound motivation:

> But whatever were gains to me I now consider loss for the sake
> of Christ. What is more, I consider everything a loss because
> of the surpassing worth of knowing Christ Jesus my Lord,
> for whose sake I have lost all things. I consider them garbage,
> that I may gain Christ and be found in him, not having a
> righteousness of my own that comes from the law, but that
> which is through faith in Christ—the righteousness that comes
> from God on the basis of faith. I want to know Christ—yes,
> to know the power of his resurrection and participation in his
> sufferings.
>
> PHILIPPIANS 3:7-10

Paul didn't discount his history but put it in subjection to knowing Christ. He was still a brilliant student and a superb thinker. He didn't reject his history and training. Similarly, we don't discount our efforts, abilities, and work, but we're to realize that God gave us the ability to achieve. We must know that our identity is in Christ.

I like Paul's perspective on working hard and following Christ as evidenced in these words from Colossians:

> Whatever you do, work at it with all your heart, as working for the Lord, not for human masters, since you know that you will receive an inheritance from the Lord as a reward. It is the Lord Christ you are serving.
> COLOSSIANS 3:23-24

So, as to your history and your identity:

- Work hard.
- Acknowledge that all you have is from God.
- Find your identity in Christ, not in your accomplishments.
- Then develop a perspective on how you'll live in the fourth quarter.

The Achilles' Heel of Character

Although the Bible rarely uses terms we would translate *character*, its pages are filled with warnings and admonitions about attributes that constitute what we call character.

Character defines who a person really is. We often speak of a person as having a good or bad character. Good character is what we attempt to build in our children and also cultivate in ourselves.

In the fourth quarter, character and the Scriptures are the foundation on which we build our understanding of the present and our hope for the future.

In Romans 5, character is embedded in the context of suffering:

We also glory in our sufferings, because we know that suffering
produces perseverance; perseverance, character; and character,
hope. And hope does not put us to shame, because God's love
has been poured out into our hearts through the Holy Spirit,
who has been given to us.

ROMANS 5:3-5

Character is an inner reality that others see only in our actions and
reputation. In the fourth quarter of life, two elements that undermine godly
character are pride and anger. Pride often precedes anger. Pride causes you
to "think of yourself more highly than you ought" (Romans 12:3). This
doesn't mean we should downplay or denigrate our accomplishments, but
we should hold them in proper balance as being gifts of God. These words
of Paul have always given me perspective: "Who makes you different from
anyone else? What do you have that you did not receive? And if you did
receive it, why do you boast as though you did not?" (1 Corinthians 4:7).

Where does a person's physical attractiveness or athletic ability or
strength come from? Cosmetics, good health practices, and training can
enhance those things, but we did not create them. God did it by the
circumstances of birth and family heritage. And each can be ruined by
dissipation and neglect.

Pride is frequently the downfall of kings and leaders. The great King
Uzziah stumbled in this way: "After Uzziah became powerful, his pride
led to his downfall" (2 Chronicles 26:16). Hezekiah, one of the godliest
of Judah's kings, also fell by pride: "Hezekiah's heart was proud and he
did not respond to the kindness shown him; therefore the LORD's wrath
was on him and on Judah and Jerusalem. Then Hezekiah repented of the
pride of his heart" (2 Chronicles 32:25-26). Note that when the leader
went wrong, it affected the entire nation and city. Similarly, today, it will
affect a church, a company, a family, and you.

Solomon, in his wisdom, expressed it well: "When pride comes,
then comes disgrace, but with humility comes wisdom" (Proverbs
11:2). Also: "Pride brings a person low, but the lowly in spirit gain
honor" (Proverbs 29:23).

We instinctively don't like proud people or respond to them positively. Yet pride can sneak up so easily in our own view of ourselves. It confuses and corrupts our identity.

The antidote to pride is a realistic assessment of ourselves that produces an inner humility. Again, we don't deny or escape our achievements. We simply don't confuse them with our identity.

The other Achilles' heel of character is anger. Anger often evolves from pride. It may result from cynicism and envy. In the fourth quarter of life, pride takes on different forms as it causes us to want to be recognized and honored for what we once were. Our anger surges when no one knows, recognizes, or cares what we once were. We see others coming into the space we once occupied, often doing what we did more creatively and better. We can either rejoice with and affirm them, or we can envy them.

In my case, I gladly saw my successors doing many things differently and better. I recognized that it really was time for me to step aside, making way for younger and more capable people. By the grace of God, I did not become either envious or resentful. I was thrilled at how they led and how they met the challenges of the next steps in The Navigators. They were kind to me, keeping me informed and asking counsel.

In many secular contexts, that's often not the case. When I stepped out of my Air Force leadership role, I was honored with a great retirement ceremony inside the huge museum at Wright-Patterson Air Force Base, under the wing of a B-52 and the nose of a stealth fighter. Nice things were said. My family and friends were there to celebrate. Then it was over. Another major general replaced me, the man I'd groomed for the job. It was a good transition.

Then—silence. No one called. No one asked advice. It was as though I had no past.

That's so often the way it is in the secular world. It was no surprise to me. Yet there's the screech of silence. I'm still friends with my successors in the Air Force as well as dozens who worked with me or for me. But there's no professional connection. I suppose my pride and ego did want some of that.

My dear friend and predecessor as The Navigators' international president, Lorne Sanny, said it well: "I am a used-to-be." My rank in the Air Force, plus its privileges and status, still remains—but it's different. And it should be different. What I must guard against is pride and ego. And so must we all. We must live in the very real present. We must understand who we are both outwardly and spiritually. I'm a husband, father, grandfather, and great-grandfather. That will never change. In reality, that gives me the greatest satisfaction.

Each of us will enter the fourth quarter in a different way. Work and jobs may not have ended well. Marriages may have broken. There may be estrangement in the family. Many issues may exist that can affect how we feel in the fourth quarter.

The Dangers of Sin, Withdrawal, Freezing, and Confusion

In the fourth quarter, the biggest issues we typically face are loss of identity and loss of significance. These may lead to issues with the other four dangers we discussed earlier.

Sin is no respecter of age. We remain as vulnerable as ever. Sexual temptation still embeds itself in our minds. Unresolved issues in life and marriage will amplify in the fourth quarter. The divorce rate of men over sixty has tripled since 1960. At a time when husband and wife should be enjoying each other more, experiencing greater freedom, and especially enjoying their grandchildren, sin may still disturb us. Sin in the form of anger and resentment and even lust will rear its ugly head. I heard an old proverb: "There's no fool like an old fool." I'm no exception. Occasionally I experience crazy thoughts, and I wonder, "When am I going to grow up?" We're never exempt from temptation and sin. But hopefully we become wiser and more vigilant to counter them.

We know of friends, coworkers, and family members who do foolish things in the fourth quarter of their lives. More than ever, we need meaningful friendships and relationships at this stage of life. There's a significant danger of withdrawing. When we no longer go to work daily, we lose our major source of regular interaction. This is a time when church, volunteer work, and social engagements become so important.

In the book *Younger Next Year*, Chris Crowley writes this:

> I retired young, for what seemed like perfectly good reasons at the time, but almost at once I felt as if I'd gone off a cliff. Lonely, sad, and deeply, deeply guilty. And bear in mind, I was happily married at the time, a ski bum, which I had always dreamed of being, and I was finally going to write. Besides, I had earned enough dough to do it, so what's to feel guilty about?
>
> As I look back . . . it's clear that it was the absence of the old pack that was the problem. . . . And most of all I miss the communication and commitment.[1]

Crowley missed the challenge of camaraderie and relationships. Men, by nature, are not social animals. Most of them prefer to *do* things—work, hunt, drink, play sports. They don't often just sit around to recount their woes and inner feelings. Women do that, not men. So when their work is withdrawn, men shrivel up. Their world narrows. Many withdraw, never having learned to build friendships outside the functional context of work.

Some find their relational connections in sports. Perhaps that's part of the reason I'm still involved in the handball community. A desire for relational connections also drives me to keep engaging with my Air Force and military friends by attending monthly dinners or participating in the activities of the Air Force Association. I also keep in touch with our Navigator staff, both past and present.

All this takes effort and intentionality. For most men, connecting with other people doesn't just happen. The antidote to withdrawal in the fourth quarter is a determination to connect in the world of believers and in the secular world. The best ways to do this are to keep in touch and network with the people of your past, participate in a small discipleship and fellowship group, and seek out new avenues of involvement.

Freezing and confusion can easily sneak up on us in the fourth quarter. We need to keep learning and growing. One thing that helped me was learning to play the cello at age seventy. I'd been involved in vocal music through the years, but after our son's death, a lesion on my vocal cords altered my ability to sing well. The cello has challenged me to keep learning. In all likelihood, I'll never be a stellar performer, but it gives me great pleasure. The multiple hours of practice to become proficient does challenge me!

Confusion comes when we no longer have a clear and compelling purpose. If our finances are adequate, we may no longer have to work in a paying job. Many men, however, keep working well into their seventies and beyond. Some of the greatest discoveries in history were made by men and women over eighty. So keep going! If our sense of purpose in life has come largely from our work, we'll be in trouble when we retire or work fewer hours. I strongly believe that work is a calling, but it's not our *only* calling. When purpose disappears, depression and a lack of motivation easily invade.

But wait! There's another purpose which supersedes all others—serving others. Do you remember the Great Commandments? Love God and love your neighbor. If we set our sights on serving and helping people, it will soon put all the other callings and purposes in perspective. We don't need to look far to find people whom we can help. Start with your own family, immediate and extended. What do they need right now? How can I help them or network some help for them? What about my neighbors? Do I even know their names? What about the widows and orphans? The Bible directly mentions widows and orphans as persons we must always care for. What about expending my resources and time to help the helpless in my city or county?

If you put your mind to it, I think you'll discover many avenues of service, both direct and indirect.

All this has the potential of erasing the confusion of the fourth quarter.

Time—Our One Nonrenewable Resource

In the fourth quarter, we become acutely aware of the shortness of our remaining time in life. None of us knows when we will die, but we all know it will happen. What do we live for in this critical time of life?

Certainly, we want to use our time for God's purposes. It's not that vacations, golf, handball, and other enjoyable activities aren't useful or deserved. Family should take up a significant portion of this time of life.

My friend, attorney Greg Stephens, has made some excellent observations and suggestions regarding time. His eight conclusions are both encouraging and sobering:

- Life on earth is short.
- Earth is not our home.
- We're going to die.
- After we die, we face judgment.
- We will appear before God.
- For all of eternity, we'll either be with God or separated from Him.
- After we die, nothing material leaves the earth with us.
- When we're in heaven, the three eternals will be with us—God, His Word, and people. [2]

These are profound facts. In the fourth quarter we want to marshal our time with purpose and discipline. Invest it well—in your family, in your times of pleasure, in your relationships, and in your time with God. Don't just stumble into this time of life. Make it count as the best time of your life—with a plan that gives you freedom and purpose.

A Fourth Quarter Plan for the Future

For your personal success and fulfillment in the fourth quarter, you need a plan and steps of action. Convictions, emotions, and good intentions are useless if not married to good deeds. We don't need a to-do list or a catchy phrase to get us going. We simply need a push and a word from God.

My suggestions are simple and few:

1. *Surrender.* Surrender your image of who you were with a thankful recollection of your history and achievements. By understanding that your significance and identity will always include far more than your past, you've made a great stride forward. Your significance and identity are who you're becoming in the fourth quarter of your life. By surrendering, you'll open the door to a new future, built on what you've become and with a view to what you're becoming.

   Approach this both spiritually and practically. Go deeper with God. Understand how God has made you and prepared you for this time. The process of surrendering is more than just a quick prayer. It will require some in-depth self-examination and time with God in reflection, and possibly journaling. If you're married, ask your wife for her input and counsel. She's such a great part of this future—and has her own fourth quarter to assess and design.

2. *Be generous.* Generosity is both a mindset and an action. It will repay you with joy, peace, and satisfaction. Certainly, be generous with your money. But also be generous with yourself—your time, your energy, your knowledge, your insights, and especially your words of affirmation for people. Be generous with your wife and your family. Be generous to the causes in which you believe. (I recommend David Green's book *Giving It All Away . . . and Getting It All Back Again.*)[3]

3. *Be realistic.* Many New Year's resolutions are like castles in the sand, swept away with the first storm of reality. We cannot change the past. We cannot change our physical health or

bodies. But we can change how we think about these things and how we see ourselves into the future.

4. *Get moderate exercise.* To do anything, you first need to take care of yourself both physically and spiritually. So exercise in a way that's enjoyable and sustainable for you, and adopt a healthier diet.

5. *Assess your personal spiritual state of affairs.* Our spiritual maturity undergirds our future. If you've been in a busy career, you may not have invested in your spiritual growth as much as you knew you should have. Now's the perfect time to rectify that. Admit where you are in terms of biblical knowledge and spiritual commitment. Then begin taking steps to grow spiritually. Make simple and reachable goals. Share them with your wife and a few close friends. Develop a moderate level of accountability. Become part of some small group in your church or with your friends. It's never too late to grow spiritually.

6. Finally, *be accessible to your family.* Understand that younger family members are where you were decades ago.

I like the way my friend Terry Pierce described the phases in the fourth quarter:

The Go Phase—I still have the energy, the drive, the ability, and the opportunities to be very engaged and productive.

The Slow-Go Phase—I realize that my energy is a bit less and my drive to accomplish has waned somewhat, so I must adjust to my new reality.

The No-Go Phase—Although I don't like to contemplate it, there will be a time when health determines what we can do, and we become very dependent on others and on tending to personal and family needs.

Be an encourager. This is another way of saying that we should keep a positive attitude toward life. No one wants to be around a grumpy, cynical old man! Certainly, the younger generations are not drawn toward that kind of person.

We also need to keep informed as best we can. We need to be able to interact on issues of our day without being a doomsayer. We can give perspective but not pronouncements. Above all, we need to listen and understand. My mentor Lorne Sanny once said, "People are not so much interested in what I think but in what I think about what they are thinking." And in that process, we must affirm and encourage.

So . . . welcome to the fourth quarter! (And for some of us, we're down to the two-minute mark to win.) Never quit. Never give up.

PART FOUR

Personal Renewal
for Facing the Dangers

SPIRITUAL RENEWAL FOR THE INNER MAN

DO YOU KNOW WHAT the acronym ROTJ means? Retired on the job. Have you seen someone like that? No motivation. Can't wait until the day ends. Lifeless and looking forward to getting away from work.

This happens spiritually. A spark goes out. Motivation dies. There's little interest in God, His Word, fellowship with believers, or growing spiritually.

People don't choose to grow dull in their spiritual lives. It just happens, often through encountering the dangers we've been discussing— loss, sin, freezing, confusion, or withdrawal. Whatever the cause, the remedy is spiritual renewal. We need a rekindling of our life in Christ, a new vitality, a rebirth of spiritual fervor.

The paintings by Michelangelo in the Sistine Chapel in Rome became dull with soot and grime over the centuries. The once-bright colors were shades of gray. Through careful experimentation, experts found that when they applied a paste of solvents that was allowed to dry and then was carefully brushed away, the original colors came to life again.

If only our spiritual restoration were as simple! But more is needed than a surface fix. We need an inner restoration.

Several times my spiritual life has lost its luster and become dull. Sometimes the cause was obvious—as with the grief and depression I've described earlier. At other times, there was no discernible cause. These were the most disturbing times. Over the years, I've reflected on what has helped me be renewed. I wish I could say that there's a once-for-all solution. There isn't. Renewal is a constant process, infused periodically by concentrated times of special stimulation from God.

In his personal struggles, the apostle Paul went through many difficult times. His words in 2 Corinthians have helped me reflect on my own spiritual renewal. He says there:

> We are pressed on every side by troubles, but not crushed and broken. We are perplexed because we don't know why things happen as they do, but we don't give up and quit. We are hunted down, but God never abandons us. We get knocked down, but we get up again and keep going.
>
> 2 CORINTHIANS 4:8-9, TLB

Paul began that chapter with the observation, "Therefore, since through God's mercy we have this ministry [the ministry of the Holy Spirit], we do not lose heart" (4:1). *The Message* phrases the same passage like this: "Since God has so generously let us in on what he is doing, we're not about to throw up our hands and walk off the job just because we run into occasional hard times."

We don't lose heart. We don't give up. Why? Paul explains the reason:

> Though outwardly we are wasting away, yet inwardly we are being *renewed day by day*. . . . So we fix our eyes not on what is seen, but on what is unseen, since what is seen is temporary, but what is unseen is eternal.
>
> 2 CORINTHIANS 4:16, 18, EMPHASIS ADDED

In the New American Standard Bible, the terms *outer man* and *inner man* are used in this passage in place of *outwardly* and *inwardly*—indicating the person seen by others (your outer man) and the person you and God see (the inner man).

We can also lose focus in the good times. All is going well, so why do I need to cry out to God for help? Easy times can lull us into focusing less on God.

How is the inner man renewed? God ultimately does the renewing, but there's much we can do toward becoming more fertile ground for God to work in. Meanwhile, the external self, or outer man, becomes deeply affected by what happens internally.

Vitality

A group of Navigator leaders from around the world met for an annual discussion of our worldwide work. We observed that some individuals and our ministries in some countries seemed to plateau in terms of growth, effectiveness, and fervor. A key ingredient in that plateauing, the leaders felt, was lack of spiritual vitality. But what is spiritual vitality?

Physical Vitality

Mentally, I began comparing spiritual vitality with physical vitality. Evidences of physical vitality are resilience, energy, flexibility, and discipline. A physician will check not only for these external signs but also for internal vital signs—heart rate, blood pressure, and possibly the evidence produced by a range of blood and urine laboratory tests.

We have a national obsession with physical health. Advertisements abound that offer us quick fixes. Gyms and fitness centers spring up everywhere. Medical advances have greatly increased the average life span. More men and women live into their eighties and nineties. Throughout life, we want to be vital physically and mentally. Health foods and exercise clubs are burgeoning industries. To live longer and healthier lives, adults in every generation are increasingly focused on nutrition, natural remedies, and being physically fit. Why? They want to live. They want to be vital.

Since Mary's battle with cancer, we find that we pay much more attention to supporting our physical vitality and will make changes to do so, such as embarking on a significantly different eating lifestyle. We want to do our part to keep physically healthy. Good physical vitality then spills over into increased emotional health and vitality. But I still like an occasional doughnut.

Spiritual Vitality

We find similar patterns spiritually. What are the internal and external vital signs of a healthy believer in Christ? These are the keys to renewal. If we simply treat the outer disciplines, we may miss the real disease.

On one recent morning, I was looking forward to a relaxed day at work with no appointments. My calendar was open. Then I learned that I'd failed to record an early morning appointment, which I had already missed. And several other appointments weren't listed in my schedule. Phone calls came in that I didn't expect. The day became a nightmare. It was even worse due to my expectation of a relaxed day. Clearly, my longed-for space vanished.

Life never seems to turn out the way it should.

It's harder.

It's busier.

Relationships become less satisfying.

Marriage is rarely what we expect.

Our career seldom meets our expectations.

In short, we live on the edge with little or no margin. It's like the doctor who called his patient to say, "I have bad news. You have only twenty-four hours to live."

"Oh, that's terrible!"

"But I have even worse news."

"What could possibly be worse than having only twenty-four hours to live?"

"Well, I've been trying to call you since yesterday."

Our lives are sometimes like that. The bad news gets worse.

So often we try to solve our pressured lives with external fixes. We organize better, reestablish priorities, increase discipline, and cut out unnecessary activities. Henri Nouwen expresses what most of us feel:

One of the most obvious characteristics of our daily lives is that we are busy. We experience our days as filled with things to do, people to meet, projects to finish, letters to write, calls to make, and appointments to keep. Our lives often seem like overpacked suitcases bursting at the seams. In fact, we are almost always aware of being behind schedule. There is a nagging sense that there are unfinished tasks, unfulfilled promises, unrealized proposals. There is always something else that we should have remembered, done, or said. There are always people we did not speak to, write to, or visit. Thus, although we are very busy, we also have a lingering feeling of never really fulfilling our obligations.[1]

Nouwen goes on to describe how this affects us inwardly:

While our minds and hearts are filled with many things, and we wonder how we can live up to the expectations imposed upon us by ourselves and others, we have a deep sense of unfulfillment. While busy with and worried about many things, we seldom feel truly satisfied, at peace, or at home. A gnawing sense of being unfulfilled underlies our filled lives.[2]

We come to the point where reorganizing is futile. We need a revolution, not reorganization. That revolution is spiritual renewal in our inner lives with God. We need a new sense of peace and purpose.

How do we achieve this spiritual vitality? Jesus tells us to remember the overriding truth of our heavenly Father's full awareness of our needs and to then do this: "Seek first his kingdom and his righteousness, and all these things will be given to you as well" (Matthew 6:33).

Seek first—our priority
His kingdom—what our sovereign God wants
His righteousness—holiness of life
These things—the sustenance of life

The context in Matthew 6 is Jesus' warning against worrying about our physical needs. In verse 24, Jesus says, "You cannot serve both God and money." You cannot live with two masters. The first step in renewing the inner life is to decide to live for only one master.

But why should we make this critical decision to serve one master? The force of this verse is seeking to serve God with all your heart, soul, and mind. We want to know and serve the God of Scripture. Our ultimate purpose is to become like Christ. Paul described it like this:

You are living a brand new kind of life that is continually learning more and more of what is right, and trying constantly to be more and more like Christ who created this new life within you.
COLOSSIANS 3:10, TLB

Our goal is to know God more deeply, as we walk with His Son daily and as we're empowered by His Spirit. He then calls us not only to His kingdom but to a holy life.

The purpose of spiritual renewal is not just to feel better about ourselves but to love and serve God, experiencing a true inner transformation.

Ingredients for Renewal

But what is the process of inner renewal?

Consider the following ingredients.

Solitude—a Place to Grow

Many men find silence and solitude uncomfortable. For me, since so much of my life is spent with people, I relish time to be alone. But being alone and quiet without some activity to occupy my attention is not easy. I want to *do* something while alone—read a book, make notes, listen to music, or sort through piles of papers on my desk. To just sit in solitude is difficult.

That's precisely the problem. We're so busy, so preoccupied, so frenetic that solitude frightens us. It should not. I need it, but I find it difficult to make room for it in my schedule.

We desperately need time apart to give God space and time to work in our lives.

At the beginning of Jesus' public ministry, John the Baptist was active in denouncing sin and calling for repentance. King Herod hated and feared John, "knowing that he was a righteous and holy man" (Mark 6:20, NASB). At his wife's instigation, Herod finally had John beheaded. This sent tremors of fear throughout the community, including Jesus' disciples. Sensing this, Jesus told them, "Come away by yourselves to a secluded place and rest a while"; Mark includes this explanation: "For there were many people coming and going, and they did not even have time to eat" (6:31, NASB).

Jesus understood his disciples' need to have some space, some solitude. Even though it appears to have been short-lived, they did get away. "Come apart or you will fall apart" is a good warning.

A seed planted in the ground needs to be left alone to grow. It will die if it's constantly being uncovered to see if it's growing. Similarly, we need to be left alone to grow properly. Solitude is a place to grow.

Solitude doesn't occur naturally. It must be purposely scheduled. We need to come away from the rush of our lives to think, reflect, pray, and recharge. How often? How long? It's your decision. It depends on your personality, needs, and past experience. But I do know that you need solitude.

You might start with setting aside a four-hour morning (evenings are notoriously injected with fatigue, interruptions, and distractions). After this initial short time, I recommend trying a full day or maybe two, for example, during a weekend. I've found—as I've grown older and busier—that I now need about two days to unwind, and only then can I get a couple of days of fruitful solitude. (I'll explain more later about how to use this time of solitude. It's not just staring at a wall!)

Reflection—Essence of Cultivation

Many years ago I read a poem (author unknown) that mirrored my personal difficulty with solitude and reflection:

> We go, and keep on going,
> Until the object of the game
> Seems to be
> To go and keep on going.
> We do, and keep on doing,
> Until we do
> Without knowing—without feelings.
> Is there no time to stop and reflect?
> Is there no time to stop?
> Is there no time?
> If we stopped, would we keep on going?
> If we reflected, would we keep doing
> What we do?
> For what we have done
> And where we have gone
> Is dissolved into oblivion
> Or strung on the meaningless chain
> Of half remembered this and that
> If there is no reflection.
> In all our doing have we done anything?
> In all our going have we been anywhere?

We experience both apprehension and anticipation in solitude and reflection. We fear not knowing what to do, and we anticipate what God can do. We must break our cycles of busyness and relentless activity, no matter how worthwhile the tasks are that we perform.

What happens when we don't take time to reflect and consider our lives?

- We suffer physically, paying the price for stress and emotional fatigue.
- Our families suffer from our lack of presence and purpose.
- Our spiritual lives suffer from not allowing God to refine our lives with Him as we reflect.

Even secular management consultants almost universally affirm the need for time away to think, reflect, and refresh. Workaholics are not productive, since efficiency is dramatically reduced with long hours of work. Much has been written on the need to balance work, rest, and recreation. People flock to semi-mystical seminars on meditation and self-development. They see their desperate need for something that will relieve their emotional pain and lack of fulfillment.

What do I mean by *reflection*? Simply thinking about your life and actions in light of God and His Word. Meditating on what the Bible says. I also strongly suggest some journaling of your thoughts. Don't let that word *journaling* confuse or discourage you. I'm not talking about writing a book or *anything that anyone else will ever read*. Just jot down your thoughts. If you're wrestling with a problem, write out the facts. I find that my mind keeps chewing over anxious thoughts repeatedly. Writing them down thwarts that cycle and brings light to my thinking. (Here again I recommend *Spiritual Journaling* by Richard Peace.)

Cultivation is an agricultural word. It usually means stirring the ground around crops to let moisture and nutrients in. It also involves killing the weeds that choke growth. That's exactly what happens spiritually. Cultivation stirs up the good crop and destroys the spiritual weeds that tend to choke us.

Consider these piercing words from A. W. Tozer:

The idea of cultivation and exercise, so dear to the saints of old, has now no place in our total religious picture. It is too slow, too common. We now demand glamour and fast flowing dramatic action. A generation of Christians reared among push buttons and automatic machines is impatient of slower and less direct methods of reaching their goals. We have been trying to apply machine-age methods to our relations with God. We read our chapter, have our short devotions and rush away, hoping to make up for our deep inward bankruptcy by attending another gospel meeting or listening to another thrilling story told by a religious adventurer lately returned from afar.

The tragic results of this spirit are all about us. Shallow lives, hollow religious philosophies, the preponderance of the element of fun in gospel meetings, the glorification of men, trust in religious externalities, quasi-religious fellowships, salesmanship methods, the mistaking of dynamic personality for the power of the Spirit.[3]

Tozer strongly urges significant times of meditation and time with God to counter this mechanized spirituality. Let's take time to reflect, so that we can keep going.

The Word of God—Building Foundations

In the physical realm, vitality requires a number of fundamental building blocks, such as properly functioning organs, mechanically adequate joints, good general health of the body, and certainly proper food, which provides correct and adequate nutrition. We care for our bodies physically by supplying them with basic foods and eliminating harmful bacteria, viruses, or cancers.

Spiritually, there's only one major food group—the Word of God, the Bible. The Scriptures are food for the soul. In Scripture, God's Word is referred to as "food," "meat," "water," and "milk." This is terminology that everyone understands. An unalterable basic requirement of spiritual renewal is an inner life fed by the Scriptures.

A healthy believer hungers for the Word. "Like newborn babies, crave pure spiritual milk, so that by it you may grow up in your salvation"

(1 Peter 2:2). This statement is addressed not only to spiritual infants. For all our days, we're to have the same hunger for spiritual milk that newborn children have for their mothers' milk. This milk is to be "pure," unmixed with anything. Spiritual milk isn't reading *about* the Bible or hearing sermons but reading the Bible directly.

The word *milk* does imply basic nutrition, which must be followed by eating solid food to grow to maturity. The same principle applies to our spiritual life:

> In fact, though by this time you ought to be teachers, you need someone to teach you the elementary truths of God's word all over again. You need milk, not solid food! Anyone who lives on milk, being still an infant, is not acquainted with the teaching about righteousness. But solid food is for the mature, who by constant use have trained themselves to distinguish good from evil.
>
> HEBREWS 5:12-14

We need growth in both our understanding *and* our application of the Scriptures in order to become healthy, mature spiritual men. This is the kind of growth in Christ that Paul depicts as being "rooted and built up in him, strengthened in the faith" (Colossians 2:7).

Spiritual renewal will not come without consistent input from the Scriptures. If regular, personal study of the Word hasn't been a pattern in your life, it may be the missing ingredient in your renewal.

Prayer and Worship—Restoring the Soul

Worship is one of the most significant acts of a believer. Unfortunately, most people think of worship as only the morning worship service at a church. That's not what I mean here. As good, enjoyable, and necessary as corporate gatherings of believers are, they're still inadequate for deep spiritual renewal. Prayer and worship are needed on a personal and private basis. They're necessary ingredients in times of solitude and reflection.

Prayer and reflection will transform any dryness or simply intellectual study of the Scriptures. We desperately need the connection of mind and spirit. Listen again to A. W. Tozer:

Press on into the deep things of God. Insist upon tasting the profounder mysteries of redemption. Keep your feet on the ground, but let your heart soar as high as it will. Refuse to be average or to surrender to the chill of your spiritual environment. . . . Unless you do these things you will reach at last (and unknown to you) the bone yard of orthodoxy and be doomed to live out your days in a spiritual poverty.[4]

Our tendency to view worship primarily in a church context causes me to attempt some definitions of *worship*. The most literal definition of *worship* is reflected by the psalmist's words: "Come, let us bow down in worship, let us kneel before the LORD our Maker" (Psalm 95:6). Old Testament and New Testament words translated *worship* frequently mean to bow down, as to a sovereign king, and then to obey that king.

The English word *worship* comes from a Middle English word meaning "to ascribe worth." God, as our king, asks for such a response. He wants us to submit to His sovereignty—willingly and with a joyful heart.

A major expression of that submission is obedience. In the Old Testament, people were often motivated to submit to God's sovereignty more by the fear of Him than by His grace. In New Testament times, we submit primarily out of love, in grateful response to God's mercy and grace in Christ, yet in reverent fear of Him.

Clearly, grace, love, and fear permeate both testaments. In the Old Testament, God's love and grace are revealed constantly in His dealing with Israel. In the New Testament, fear is still present: "It is a fearful thing to fall into the hands of the living God" (Hebrews 10:31, KJV). "Since you call on a Father who judges each person's work impartially, live out your time as foreigners here in reverent fear" (1 Peter 1:17).

We often think of worship as an experience—something we do formally or informally to praise God or to quietly meditate on His grandeur. But in addition to these notions, I see two contrasting and complementary aspects of worship:

1. To subject ourselves to the sovereignty of God
2. To respond to God's love with adoration and praise

Both aspects can be observed in the story of Job. Job's response to overwhelming tragedy in his life was to express his grief (tear his robe, shave his head), repent, and worship—allowing God's sovereignty to reign over every part of his life:

Then he fell to the ground in worship and said:

> "Naked I came from my mother's womb,
>   and naked I will depart.
> The Lord gave and the Lord has taken away;
>   may the name of the Lord be praised."

JOB 1:20-21

Both in public and in private, we need to bow down (symbolically, or by kneeling or bowing) as we express our adoration and praise.

The book of Revelation shows us vivid scenes of perfect worship:

The twenty-four elders fall down before him who sits on the throne and worship him who lives for ever and ever. They lay their crowns before the throne and say:

> "You are worthy, our Lord and God,
>   to receive glory and honor and power."

REVELATION 4:10-11

And they sang a new song, saying:

"You are worthy to take the scroll
and to open its seals,
because you were slain,
and with your blood you purchased for God
persons from every tribe and language and
people and nation."

REVELATION 5:9

Then I looked and heard the voice of many angels, numbering thousands upon thousands, and ten thousand times ten thousand. They encircled the throne and the living creatures and the elders. In a loud voice they were saying:

"Worthy is the Lamb, who was slain,
to receive power and wealth and wisdom and strength
and honor and glory and praise!"

REVELATION 5:11-12

This is an incredible picture of worship, and it can make any expression of worship this side of heaven seem insignificant. Christ is clearly the focus—God-become-man, who was slain and who lives forever. The picture brings to mind the Psalms, where worship often involves praise, singing, thanksgiving, verbal submission, and bowing down before God.

As we await this magnificent scene in heaven, what is our worship today? It certainly includes some of the same expressions when believers meet together—praise, singing, thanksgiving, verbal submission, and bowing. Yet often the emphasis is more personal, more inward, and less formal. It takes place wherever believers are located—alone or together—not only in a temple or sanctuary. As Jesus said, "True worshipers will worship the Father in the Spirit and in truth" (John 4:23).

Worship is attributing worth to God with reverence and awe. We focus on God, and we give ourselves to Him through prayer, singing, praise, and obeying—we worship *in spirit*. In these activities, our guide is Scripture. We worship *in truth*. These elements of worship—prayer, singing, praise, and obedience—apply both to our private worship and to worship in community (church meetings or other gatherings of believers). Perhaps we should more often physically bow down, affirming our submission to a holy God.

We have great freedom in our expressions of worship. Some prefer quietness or soft music. Some celebrate with clapping and lively songs. Others prefer a traditional liturgy. In this we learn to serve one another—new and mature believers, from different cultures and customs—by deferring to others' expressions of worship as we remember that God looks on the heart.

In your solitude, learn to pray and praise in your worship. It will renew your spirit. I urge this, but I openly admit that it's difficult for me as a doer. It requires more discipline than most of my activities.

Fellowship and Friendship—the Encouragement Factor

We need other people. We cannot be loners and expect to grow spiritually. As much as men may think that we can get along by ourselves, we'll soon wither and die spiritually without other people. Being a believer in Christ is not an individual sport. We're inextricably connected to others in the body of Christ.

All my earlier discussions of friendship and accountability fit here. Paul found that he desperately needed others. At one point, when he was down emotionally, he was encouraged by Titus: "But God, who comforts the depressed, comforted us by the coming of Titus" (2 Corinthians 7:6, NASB). Paul needed Titus for his renewal, which is in line with the relational truths we're taught in the book of Proverbs:

- A man's counsel is sweet to his friend. Do not forsake your own friend or your father's friend. (27:9-10, NASB)
- Iron sharpens iron, so one man sharpens another. (27:17, NASB)
- As in water face reflects face, so the heart of man reflects man. (27:19, NASB)

Something profound happens in the context of heart-to-heart fellowship!

In the New Testament, we see that our intimate relationship with Jesus and our faithfulness to Him requires us to "consider how to stimulate one another to love and good deeds, not forsaking our own assembling together . . . but encouraging one another" (Hebrews 10:24-25, NASB). We need other believers. Men especially need other men who will stimulate their souls' thirst for God. Some men will make you hunger for money or success. Some will talk sports and politics, making you want to learn more about these things. But we need a context of fellowship where the conversation is about important matters of the Spirit.

Solitude should not replace fellowship. In fact, there are times when getting apart with two to five other people for the purpose of seeking God can be tremendously encouraging in our renewal. For instance, a day apart—spending brief times in prayer and discussion with other men along with personal times in the Word and reflection—can greatly help someone who's new to these sorts of things. I've noticed an increase in people going on personal spiritual retreats with a mentor, a "spiritual director," to help them use the time profitably. Get the help you need to grow.

Inner Application—Obedience of the Heart

All this time in solitude, reflection, the Word, worship, and fellowship will be of little meaning unless there's practical application in our lives. Later we'll discuss outward obedience. But outward obedience depends upon the prior application of Christlikeness to our inner person.

As adults, most of us have learned to externally control our baser instincts. We hold in our anger, we guard how we express our attitudes, and we check our emotional responses. Yet the inner person may hardly change at all. The most profound effect of the Spirit's work in our lives takes place in the inner person. He wants to move us—beginning with our character and attitudes—toward Christlikeness.

The dangerous issues of sin we've discussed have their roots in the inner person. Real spiritual renewal will take place when we change our attitudes of pride, egotism, jealousy, and contentiousness. We need to change how we think about life, ourselves, people, and circumstances. Paul said, "Have this attitude in yourselves which was also in Christ Jesus" (Philippians 2:5, NASB). This instruction comes in the context of Paul's pointing out Jesus' total lack of selfishness and conceit, His willingness to give up His own interests.

Earlier I discussed anger extensively, and as a reminder—since this is an Achilles' heel for so many men—I particularly recommend that you deal with any anger that's deeply rooted in your inner person.

Inner application means taking control of your thought life. This certainly includes thoughts of sex and lust. But it's far more than that. It includes how we think about people, circumstances, and God Himself. We're to take "every thought captive to the obedience of Christ" (2 Corinthians 10:5, NASB).

Inner application most fundamentally means listening to the Holy Spirit as you read the Word, reflect, and pray. The Spirit will point out issues in your inner life. When He does, ask God to change you, and do all you can to be obedient.

SPIRITUAL RENEWAL FOR THE OUTER MAN

A DEEP SPIRITUAL ILLNESS occurs when our inner and outer persons are incompatible. We cannot long stand the tension of believing one way and living another. We either change beliefs to match our actions, or we change our actions to match our beliefs.

Renewal begins inside our hearts. It is completed by an external conformity to God's plan for us.

Inner vitality without outer vitality results in a useless life. Outer vitality without inner vitality results in a hypocritical, two-faced life. Inner vitality plus outer vitality gives real spiritual power to our lives.

Biblical Clues to External Spiritual Vitality

I don't want to invent or prescribe a checklist for external spiritual vitality, but I do believe some clues are helpful.

The epistle of James is the classic biblical statement on our external life—our good works, as it's called. The Bible speaks well for itself, so

I'll elaborate only briefly on the instruction of James. His basic thesis of the relationship between works and faith is expressed this way:

> What good is it, my brothers and sisters, if someone claims to have faith but has no deeds? Can such faith save them? Suppose a brother or a sister is without clothes and daily food. If one of you says to them, "Go in peace; keep warm and well fed," but does nothing about their physical needs, what good is it? In the same way, faith by itself, if it is not accompanied by action, is dead.
> But someone will say, "You have faith; I have deeds."
> Show me your faith without deeds, and I will show you my faith by my deeds.
> JAMES 2:14-18

What can help us develop external spiritual vitality?

Develop a Heart for God

A godly man having a heart for God means that his desire for God is acted upon through a regular, meaningful devotional life and times of prayer:

> Come near to God and he will come near to you. Wash your hands, you sinners, and purify your hearts, you double-minded. . . . Humble yourselves before the Lord, and he will lift you up.
> JAMES 4:8, 10

In our daily times with Him, we draw near to Him in the Word and prayer.

Know and Apply God's Word

It's so easy to know the Scriptures well and still not apply them to our lives. It's what many would call *hypocrisy*. We want to grow deeply in God's Word, but we must also allow it to change our lives. James communicates this clearly:

Do not merely listen to the word, and so deceive yourselves. Do what it says. Anyone who listens to the word but does not do what it says is like someone who looks at his face in a mirror and, after looking at himself, goes away and immediately forgets what he looks like. But whoever looks intently into the perfect law that gives freedom, and continues in it—not forgetting what they have heard, but doing it—they will be blessed in what they do.

JAMES 1:22-25

God has little time for the man who knows much and does little.

Control Your Tongue

The godly man controls his tongue. "Those who consider themselves religious and yet do not keep a tight rein on their tongues deceive themselves, and their religion is worthless" (James 1:26).

James also tells us this:

We all stumble in many ways. Anyone who is never at fault in what they say is perfect, able to keep their whole body in check.

When we put bits into the mouths of horses to make them obey us, we can turn the whole animal. Or take ships as an example. Although they are so large and are driven by strong winds, they are steered by a very small rudder wherever the pilot wants to go. Likewise, the tongue is a small part of the body, but it makes great boasts. Consider what a great forest is set on fire by a small spark. The tongue also is a fire, a world of evil among the parts of the body. It corrupts the whole body, sets the whole course of one's life on fire, and is itself set on fire by hell.

All kinds of animals, birds, reptiles and sea creatures are being tamed and have been tamed by mankind, but no human being can tame the tongue. It is a restless evil, full of deadly poison.

JAMES 3:2-8

We know that the mouth speaks whatever is in the heart. Which of us hasn't been deeply embarrassed by the way our words revealed our heart? Notice that in this passage James reminds us, "No human being can tame the tongue." The implication is that only God can change us inwardly so that what comes off our tongues reveals a heart for God.

Ask God to help you become such a man.

Act Honorably toward Others

The godly man treats every person with honor, grace, and respect.

> My dear friends, don't let public opinion influence how you live out our glorious, Christ-originated faith. If a man enters your church wearing an expensive suit, and a street person wearing rags comes in right after him, and you say to the man in the suit, "Sit here, sir; this is the best seat in the house!" and either ignore the street person or say, "Better sit here in the back row," haven't you segregated God's children and proved that you are judges who can't be trusted?
>
> Listen, dear friends. Isn't it clear by now that God operates quite differently? He chose the world's down-and-out as the kingdom's first citizens, with full rights and privileges. This kingdom is promised to anyone who loves God. And here you are abusing these same citizens! Isn't it the high and mighty who exploit you, who use the courts to rob you blind?
>
> JAMES 2:1-6, MSG

Have you ever been slighted or treated badly because you were a "nobody"? The memory of that slight ought to remind us to treat everyone as though they were Christ's personal representatives.

Develop Humility and Christlike Ambition

The godly man subdues anger, factions, and strife in a spirit of humility:

My dear brothers and sisters, take note of this: Everyone should
be quick to listen, slow to speak and slow to become angry,
because human anger does not produce the righteousness that
God desires.

Who is wise and understanding among you? Let them
show it by their good life, by deeds done in the humility that
comes from wisdom. But if you harbor bitter envy and selfish
ambition in your hearts, do not boast about it or deny the
truth. Such "wisdom" does not come down from heaven but
is earthly, unspiritual, demonic. For where you have envy and
selfish ambition, there you find disorder and every evil practice.

What causes fights and quarrels among you? Don't they
come from your desires that battle within you?

JAMES 1:19-20; 3:13-16; 4:1

Our inner spiritual lives are often defined by what causes us to get
angry. Our inner lusts and ambitions are revealed by the conflicts and
quarrels we generate.

Resist Sin and Evil

The godly man actively resists sin and the evil one.

Submit yourselves, then, to God. Resist the devil, and he will
flee from you. Come near to God and he will come near to
you. Wash your hands, you sinners, and purify your hearts, you
double-minded.

JAMES 4:7-8

We must allow no compromise with sin. We must resist the temptation. Never allow the enemy a foothold in your life or spirit, and your
external walk will reflect a pure heart. This requires work and effort.

Stay Accountable in Relationships and Fellowship

The godly man is active in fellowship with other believers.

Therefore confess your sins to each other and pray for each other so that you may be healed. The prayer of a righteous person is powerful and effective.

Elijah was a human being, even as we are. He prayed earnestly that it would not rain, and it did not rain on the land for three and a half years. Again he prayed, and the heavens gave rain, and the earth produced its crops.

My brothers and sisters, if one of you should wander from the truth and someone should bring that person back, remember this: Whoever turns a sinner from the error of their way will save them from death and cover over a multitude of sins.

JAMES 5:16-20

We need one another for lasting spiritual renewal.

The spiritually renewed person demonstrates discipline, good conduct, a good reputation, and a depth of knowledge of the Scripture.

Walking in the Spirit

What role does the Holy Spirit play in our spiritual renewal? The Spirit is the star, the major player. God the Father sovereignly rules over all. God the Son, sent by the Father, died for our sins and now reigns in heaven. God the Holy Spirit was sent to be the indwelling presence of the Father and Son in the believer. The Spirit was sent following Christ's ascension.

Many believers can be uncomfortable with discussions about the Holy Spirit. Those in charismatic denominations see the Spirit in many external signs, such as tongues, healing, and prophecy. Those in noncharismatic denominations see the Spirit in more quiet intercessory ways. Either emphasis can easily miss some of the primary purposes of the Holy Spirit.

The following passages highlight a single key truth:

- Walk by the Spirit, and you will not carry out the desire of the flesh. (Galatians 5:16, NASB)

- If we live by the Spirit, let us also walk by the Spirit. (Galatians 5:25, NASB)
- Do not get drunk with wine, for that is dissipation, but be filled with the Spirit. (Ephesians 5:18, NASB)

We are to walk by the Spirit, live by the Spirit, and be filled and controlled by the Spirit. I will not and cannot solve the conflicting views of the charismatic gifts of the Spirit. That discussion clouds the primary thrust of the Holy Spirit's work.

Before entering a direct discussion about walking in the Spirit, note the work that the Holy Spirit has already done in us.

- *We are regenerated by the Spirit.* "Very truly I tell you, no one can enter the kingdom of God unless they are born of water and the Spirit. Flesh gives birth to flesh, but the Spirit gives birth to spirit" (John 3:5-6).

- *We are indwelt by the Spirit.* "You, however, are not in the realm of the flesh but are in the realm of the Spirit, if indeed the Spirit of God lives in you. And if anyone does not have the Spirit of Christ, they do not belong to Christ. . . . And if the Spirit of him who raised Jesus from the dead is living in you, he who raised Christ from the dead will also give life to your mortal bodies because of his Spirit who lives in you" (Romans 8:9-11).

- *We're sealed by the Spirit.* "Do not grieve the Holy Spirit of God, with whom you were sealed for the day of redemption" (Ephesians 4:30).

- *We're baptized into one body by the Spirit.* "Just as a body, though one, has many parts, but all its many parts form one body, so it is with Christ. For we were all baptized by one Spirit so as to form one body—whether Jews or Gentiles, slave or free—and we were all given the one Spirit to drink" (1 Corinthians 12:12-13).

If all this is true, then why aren't we always spiritual people? Why don't we always experience a life in the Spirit that is marked by peace, joy, hope, and love?[1]

The answer is not all that complicated. In fact, the Scriptures are clear. Let's consider these three phrases as keys:

- *Grieve not . . .*
- *Quench not . . .*
- *Walk in . . .*

Do Not Grieve the Holy Spirit

Look at the context of this command—and it is a command:

> Therefore each of you must put off falsehood and speak truthfully to your neighbor, for we are all members of one body. "In your anger do not sin": Do not let the sun go down while you are still angry, and do not give the devil a foothold. Anyone who has been stealing must steal no longer, but must work, doing something useful with their own hands, that they may have something to share with those in need.
>
> Do not let any unwholesome talk come out of your mouths, but only what is helpful for building others up according to their needs, that it may benefit those who listen. And do not grieve the Holy Spirit of God, with whom you were sealed for the day of redemption. Get rid of all bitterness, rage and anger, brawling and slander, along with every form of malice. Be kind and compassionate to one another, forgiving each other, just as in Christ God forgave you.
>
> EPHESIANS 4:25-32

The context is sin! *Sin* grieves the Holy Spirit. A key to the Spirit-filled life is to deal quickly with any sin of the present or past, no matter how small or great it may seem to us.

When we tolerate unconfessed sin, we cause deep sorrow to the Holy Spirit.

Do Not Quench the Spirit

Again, note the context:

> Be cheerful no matter what; pray all the time; thank God no matter what happens. This is the way God wants you who belong to Christ Jesus to live.
>
> Don't suppress the Spirit, and don't stifle those who have a word from the Master. On the other hand, don't be gullible. Check out everything, and keep only what's good. Throw out anything tainted with evil.
>
> 1 THESSALONIANS 5:16-22, MSG

The warning not to smother or suppress or quench the Spirit is surrounded by exhortations about rejoicing, praying constantly, giving thanks, listening, and carefully examining messages from God through other people. To quench the Holy Spirit is to say no to Him and His work.

I believe the Spirit is communicating to us almost continuously. Have you ever experienced the sense that you ought to do something—call a friend, talk to someone, drive somewhere, or do something? As we walk in the Spirit, we sense God tugging at our hearts.

So often I've ignored those tugs. I've thought, *I don't have time. It's not important. I'm just imagining things.* We have many excuses for not listening to the Spirit's quiet whispers.

One time I was leaving a meeting at our Glen Eyrie Conference Center; I'd wanted to talk with someone afterward, but he was busy. So I drove toward home. I suddenly had the sense that I should go back. I ignored it and drove as I struggled. I wanted to go home. Finally, I turned back and obeyed the urging of the Spirit. I was able to find the person for a significant conversation.

Many people have told of being awakened in the night to pray for a person or to call someone, only to find that a crisis was going on in that person's life. Many times I've been traveling by plane trying to get some work done, desperately trying to ignore the person seated next to me. But then God nudged me to start a conversation—and it led to that person receiving Christ or sharing with me a deep need.

Quenching the Spirit also occurs when we willfully disobey something the Scriptures clearly tell us to do.

Walk in the Spirit

The Greek word translated "walk" (NASB) is different in Galatians 5:16 and 5:25. In verse 16, it is *peripateō*, a normal word for "walk." In this context, it means to tread all around or to walk about in the company of the Spirit in order to avoid being influenced by the flesh. Just as a child (or even a teenager) walking with parents is far less likely to get in trouble than if he or she is alone, so it is in our walking with the Spirit. If we're continually aware of the Spirit's presence, we'll resist the flesh.

In verse 25, the word translated "walk" is *stoicheō*, meaning "to march in rank," "to keep step," or "to walk by rule." It's connected to the phrase "if we live by the Spirit." So we could say, *Since we have the source of spiritual life by the Holy Spirit, let us also conduct ourselves according to the rule of the Spirit.*

Both *The Living Bible* and *The Message* give enlightening paraphrases of this verse:

- If we are living now by the Holy Spirit's power, let us follow the Holy Spirit's leading in every part of our lives. (TLB)

- Since this is the kind of life we have chosen, the life of the Spirit, let us make sure that we do not just hold it as an idea in our heads or a sentiment in our hearts, but work out its implications in every detail of our lives. (MSG)

Again, the context is crucial. In Galatians 5:13-15, the apostle Paul speaks of our relationships to one another, how we should love our neighbors as ourselves. He warns against angry conflict. He then lists detailed works of the flesh (5:17-21)—sexual immorality, witchcraft, relational sins, and bad moral conduct. Then in 5:22-23, Paul lists the familiar fruit of the Spirit. To "keep in step with the Spirit" is the key to not yielding to the pull of the fleshly life (5:25). Walking in the Spirit is a day-by-day, hour-by-hour, step-by-step relationship with the Holy Spirit.

Grieve not, quench not, walk—these are the steps to living according to the Spirit. These are the keys to true spiritual renewal.

In his writings, Oswald Chambers spoke often of the role of the Holy Spirit in our lives, as in this passage:

> The one and only characteristic of the Holy Ghost in a man is a strong family likeness to Jesus Christ, and freedom from everything that is unlike Him. Are we prepared to set ourselves apart for the Holy Spirit's ministrations in us?

> The Holy Spirit cannot be located as a Guest in a house. He invades everything. . . . He takes charge of everything, my part is to walk in the light and to obey all that He reveals.[2]

We Cannot Always Avoid Danger

We've looked carefully throughout this book at five critical areas of danger that *every man* will face. You are not exempt from those dangers—and neither am I. We must be on guard.

Yet at some point, each of us will fail. I've tried to remind you throughout this book that God can and will show compassion, mercy, and forgiveness to any man when he fails, or falls, or merely slips a bit. The following story should remind us all how the renewal process can be appropriated.

One day it happened. And what was this "it"?

The man's mind wandered back over the past several years. His life as a believer had started quite clearly. There was no question of that conscious decision he made to believe in Christ. He remembered his hunger for the Scriptures, for discovering this newfound faith and seeing it transform his marriage, his family, his work.

Then—slowly, slowly—a deadening routine began to creep in. He kept doing all the things that he knew he should: reading Scripture, attending church activities, and participating in a small fellowship group, all the accoutrements of a committed believer. He couldn't quite identify when a spiritual dullness entered his life. But he saw himself becoming more self-centered, more irritable, more distant in his relationships.

He noticed the excitement of a few friends who were younger in their faith. There was a fleeting thought: *I wonder where my excitement went?* But it was just that—a fleeting thought. He'd found that if he became too introspective, too many unanswerable and troubling questions came up. He was simply too busy to let his emotions be stirred up with doubts.

He mentioned some of these feelings to a friend. The reply: "Don't worry about it. You're doing okay. Just press on and trust God."

Well, that was what he was trying to do. So he kept pressing on.

But soon, even his spiritual routine failed to salve his conscience. He began to feel hypocritical. He was becoming like some of the back-pew church attenders he'd so soundly criticized in his young fervor. He frightened himself when he recognized that he really didn't care too much about anything spiritual. After a summer hiatus from his Bible study group, he decided not to rejoin. He was busy at work. His kids needed more of his time for Little League and school activities. His quiet time became more sporadic.

He knew something was wrong. But he hadn't been unfaithful to his wife, and there were no overt sins in his life. He kept trudging along. But it was starting to affect him emotionally. He didn't sleep well. He began to resent his wife's spiritual growth. He found himself becoming more irri-table with her. He resented the emotional distance between them, espe-cially since they'd prided themselves on being able to talk about anything.

Late in the year, he was hurriedly trying to catch up on his annual commitment, doggedly determining to read through the Bible. Suddenly, a phrase in Revelation 2:4 pierced his heart: "You have forsaken the love you had at first." Something began to happen in his mind and heart. He didn't sleep well that night. *Has that happened to me? Have I lost my first love for Christ?* He began asking God to show him if this was his problem.

Over the next three weeks, as he thought and prayed, several things became clear.

He realized that he'd allowed specific issues of pride to slip into his life. Some of it was what he thought of as spiritual pride. He remembered his reaction when he failed to get the promotion at work. Though at the time he thought he'd handled it reasonably well, he now saw that it left a wound that hadn't healed. He remembered a resentment against God—and against a coworker who got the promotion.

The Spirit of God brought several other issues to his mind. He jotted them down in the beginnings of a private journal. He prayed over each issue or incident as God brought it to his mind. He asked for forgiveness. A couple of times he even wept—which really wasn't his style.

Over the next three months, he sensed signs of—well, for lack of a better term, *renewal.*

He finally revealed some of this to a friend he'd been avoiding for the past year. His friend listened carefully, then said, "I've seen something slipping spiritually in your life. I didn't know what it was. In fact, you may recall that I broached the subject after a workout at the athletic club. I remember you put up a pretty clear No Trespassing sign. So I just continued to pray for you that God would pursue you for whatever was needed." They agreed to meet weekly to talk and pray.

The man decided finally to take a weekend away—by himself—to spend with God. He took along only his Bible, his journal notes, and a couple of books his friend had recommended to stimulate his thinking. His time away was both a struggle and a significant spiritual experience.

Now, a month later, he realized that he was like a new man. He sensed a deeper commitment to the lordship of Christ. He had a renewed love for God.

It was happening—a really deep spiritual renewal. It didn't happen in a single day. But one day he seemed to fully realize that God had been faithful to him and that he'd responded to God over a period of several months.

He finally felt as if he'd faced several spiritual dangers—and had emerged a different person.

A Final Word

We can look at these dangers as creating a hard, frightening, and risky journey. Or, we can see them as an adventure of seeking God in the midst of real life. I prefer the adventure. Take on the new experience of creativity and discovery as you navigate an exciting life with God, your wife, your family, and your friends.

Approach loss, sin, freezing, confusion, and withdrawal like someone who was just given a map of an unknown wilderness and is now equipped to find the way forward. Facing these dangers will make you stronger, more agile, and more resilient.

Dangers abound in living out the life of Christ, but there are warning signs and help from God at every turn. We want to finish life well as men. We want to be role models to our children and to the nonbelieving world. We want to live in peace and joy in the midst of a world that pressures us at every point. We can avoid the dangers if we heed the signs and carefully apply the antidotes we've discussed.

Have a great trip along this road of life!

Bible Study and Discussion Guide

EVERY BOOK ON SPIRITUAL LIFE should be viewed through the lens of Scripture. It will stand or fall depending on whether it expresses conceptual and practical truths in light of biblical doctrine led by the illumination of the Holy Spirit. Everything discussed in this book is incomplete, with much more to be said and much more that could be grounded in the truth of Scripture.

This study and discussion guide for *Dangers Men Face* is meant to help you go far beyond what I've written. In personal stories and group discussion, the Holy Spirit will aid you in your understanding. Such discussion is central to the purpose of community and *ecclēsia* ("church" or "assembly").

This study is built around eight times of discussion. You may want to extend some of the lessons to two sessions for a longer series of total sessions.

Make it fun! Bring in some humor as you relate your reactions to the Scriptures, ideas, and concepts. Challenge one another. Above all, make the discussion personal and practical, not just theoretical. Pick holes in my thinking in the text of the book. Challenge the concepts. God, by His Spirit, will give you insight and understanding. Jesus is our model and the one who paved the way for our salvation. He is the author of new life here and eternal life to come.

I strongly suggest that you discuss the indicated Scripture passages along with the concepts presented in the book.

Study 1

Chapters 1–3

Your goal here is to discuss and understand the concept of *dangers* and to introduce and relate to the specific danger of loss.

Scripture Discovery: Read Acts 27:1–28:10 and 1 Peter 5:8-9.

1. In Acts 27 and 28, what were the dangers Paul encountered? How aware was he of the dangers? What principles can you deduce from how Paul faced them?

_____

_____

_____

2. In 1 Peter 5:8-9, what's the danger? How are we to react?

_____

_____

_____

3. How would you define *danger*? Give an example of an encounter with danger and how you got through it. What did you learn from the experience? Discuss how some dangers are more subtle and less easily detected.

_____

_____

4. Discuss the difference between physical and spiritual dangers.

_____

_____

Loss

In this book, several types of loss are discussed. The general idea of loss is taken for granted. The saying "You win some, you lose some" typifies sports. But life is not a game. Some losses are devastating, and some are just part of the normal ups and downs of life.

5. Discuss the general idea of loss. What was the first devastating loss that you remember experiencing? What other losses, big or small, have a strong place in your memory? What was your reaction to each one? What was the long-term effect of the loss?

6. What emotions have you experienced in dealing with losses?

As the first example of loss, consider loss of motivation.

7. How do you define *motivation*? Give an example of someone who seems strongly motivated and an example of someone who seems to lack motivation.

8. What does chapter 3 describe as the greatest motivator?

9. Why are desires, even good desires, insufficient to keep us motivated for a lifetime?

10. What part does fear play in motivation? Is it a legitimate motivator?

11. Share some meaningful quotes from chapter 3 that helped you.

12. How are purpose and motivation related? Consider Philippians 1:12-26.

_____

_____

13. List one or two things you can do now to be motivated or to build a proper base for motivation.

_____

_____

14. What one thing do you think you should do or change in your life as a result of this study?

_____

_____

Study 2

Chapters 4–8

Loss of motivation can be somewhat intangible. Loss of position strikes you immediately. It brings loss of influence, significance, identity, and confidence. Not everyone experiences all of these, but we all experience some of them in varying degrees. (You may want to take two sessions to delve into these losses more deeply.)

Scripture Discovery: Read Ephesians 1:1-14, Philippians 2:5-11, and 1 Corinthians 4:7.

1. Most believers understand theologically that our ultimate identity rests in being a child of God and growing to be more like Christ. Define what this means from the passages above.

_____

_____

2. What does this look like in practice?

_____

_____

3. Why is a loss of position inevitable? What are some responses—both good and bad—you're facing or will face in losing your position? (Check out the decision of Ahithophel in 2 Samuel 17:23.)

4. Why is so much of our value and identity as men derived from work?

5. How would you define *influence*? What is its source? How is influence destroyed?

6. What's the difference between influence and identity? What are common ways we view identity in ourselves or others? When does our identity help or hinder us?

7. Describe what "identity in Christ" means and what it means to you personally.

8. Describe a confident person. How is confidence built? How is it lost? Give examples.

9. Where do we often place our confidence? Compare that to having confidence in God.

The Antidote for Loss

We easily recognize these losses and have faced many of them. But now we need to investigate how to either restore confidence or build a different foundation for our confidence. Simply saying "I put my confidence in God" doesn't make it so. "I submit my losses to God" is easy to say but not so easy to do.

An antidote cures something that is wrong; it counters the effects of wrong thinking or wrong decisions that we may encounter in the unexpected events that we call losses.

10. In the discussion on Philippians 3 in chapter 8, Paul's solutions were listed. Discuss that process as it applies to your own personal losses.

_____

_____

11. How can loss in life lead to a more intimate walk with Christ? Connect this to God's sovereignty. Share what you've discerned regarding God's purposes in your losses.

_____

_____

12. Consider these statements from chapter 8: "I cannot control my circumstances, but I can control my response. . . . The key to living victoriously with loss is how I respond *over time*." In your opinion and from your experience, is this true or not true? Describe how this has worked or not worked in your life.

_____

_____

Study 3

Chapters 9–10

No one likes to talk about sin, unless perhaps it's the sins of other people. Sin and evil form the root of the world's problems. But personal sin is what troubles us most. God provided the remedy for the penalty for sin through Jesus. He died for our sin. Yet we keep sinning. Sin doesn't disappear from our mortal lives. We acknowledge that fact while wrestling with it daily. It becomes especially dangerous to us when we allow it to sneak up on us or when we excuse its pervasiveness in our lives, failing to recognize it and deal with it.

In this study we'll consider sin in the broader sense and then in the specifics of the sexual aspects of our lives.

Scripture Discovery: Read Galatians 5:20-21; Romans 4:22–5:1; 5:12-18; 6:6-7; and Proverbs 7:6-27.

1. Summarize the major teaching from the Galatians and Romans passages. How does sin (singular) differ from sins (plural)?

   _____

   _____

   _____

2. What does it mean to finish life well? Why does it seem so hard to do? How does sin creep in and keep us from finishing the race of life well?

   _____

   _____

   _____

3. Why do we keep committing sin even when we're "dead to sin"?

   _____

   _____

4. What is your strategy for finishing your life well? Don't be discouraged if you don't have one. It took me some time to think this through—and it's still in process. What are some steps you can take now for this strategy?

   _____

   _____

   _____

Sexual Temptation

5. Why is sexual temptation such a difficult issue for men to discuss?

6. Sexual temptation outside marriage has always been present. How has the accessibility of pornography affected the level of danger?

7. Discuss your experience with pornography. Share what you personally do to combat this temptation in your own life and family. Almost every man has seen pornography at some time in his life. How did it affect you?

8. Review the letter in chapter 10. Discuss the solutions it proposes.

9. What's the motivation for not yielding to sexual temptation?

10. Whether or not you are currently engaged in viewing pornography, what steps will you take to stay away from pornography in the future?

Study 4

Chapters 11–14

It's fair to ask why I isolated the particular sins related to sexual temptation, conflict, anger, and pride. The simple answer is that they are the ones that I've observed affect men the most. I could have included envy, jealousy, gossip, ambition, greed, and more. You may want to add these to the discussion.

We know that sin destroys us. Even though our salvation from the penalty of sin is assured, we still battle sin daily. The process of sanctification leads us to a deeper, holier life. It's an ongoing process till the day we die.

By dealing with the specific sins in these chapters, you'll be led to confront other sins as well. We all want to live righteous, holy lives. This study will help you in that process.

Scripture Discovery: Read Romans 6–7 and Psalm 51.

1. What surprised you as you read of Paul's struggle with sin in chapters 6 and 7 of Romans? Continuing the discussion from the previous lesson, how do Romans 6:11-23 and 7:24–8:2 help you understand the perverse power of sin?

2. Psalm 51 deals with more than David's sin with Bathsheba. What principles can you glean from this psalm?

Conflict

3. When does conflict become sinful? How does unresolved conflict regularly afflict you and the body of Christ? How does unresolved conflict affect your relationship with God?

4. Read Galatians 5 and compare verses 22-23 with verses 19-21. Where does conflict and the resolution of conflict fit in these verses?

5. In any given conflict, we may be legitimately injured and therefore led to believe that we have the "high ground" in a claim against the offending party. Can you forgive someone who has wronged you while holding on to your rights at the same time? How does insistence on getting your own way hinder spiritual growth? See Matthew 18:15-22 and Luke 17:3-4.

Anger

Read Proverbs 29:11, Ecclesiastes 7:9, and James 3.

6. You may have grown up with parents who were often angry. How did that affect you? What emotions did you feel? (If you didn't experience this, consider how you would answer if you did.)

7. How have you experienced and dealt with anger in your life? Identify some of the worst times.

8. What do you do when you're angry with God? Can we experience anger toward God without it being sin? Is it ever okay to express anger toward God?

_____

_____

9. What happens when we fail to recognize and deal with anger in our lives?

_____

_____

Pride

Read 1 Peter 5:1-6, Philippians 2:5-13, and Proverbs 6:16-19.

10. What are some evidences of pride? When you see them in yourself or in others, how do you feel?

_____

_____

11. What's the difference between sinful pride and being proud of your own accomplishments or those of your children or grandchildren?

_____

_____

The Antidote for Sin

12. How are cancer and sin alike?

_____

_____

_____

13. What is confession? How public should it be?

_____

_____

_____

14. What does accountability look like for you? How can you gain more accountability?

_____

_____

_____

_____

15. Why does healing from sin often take a long time? How complete will healing be? What lessons can you learn from David's sin in 2 Samuel 11–12 and from his confession in Psalm 51? How could David still be called "a man after God's own heart" after having committed these sins?

_____

_____

_____

_____

_____

Study 5

Chapters 15–17

The next three dangers may seem less threatening after the heavy discussions on loss and sin. Freezing, confusion, and withdrawal don't seem as obvious as the other dangers. They may seem almost invisible to you and to others. There's no fever or physical illness to herald their presence. They're not as obviously devastating as loss and sin. Yet their insidious effect is the seedbed of profound emotional trauma and debilitation—a fact that you may not have thought of before. (I guarantee you that such things as these will invade your life at some point.)

Scripture Discovery: Read 2 Corinthians 5:17 and Proverbs 1:5, 12:1, and 18:15.

Freezing

1. Restate the concept of freezing from your perspective. Describe some people you know who seem to have frozen.

2. What helps us to continue growing and developing mentally and in other ways? What scriptural basis do you see for growing and not freezing?

3. What motivates you to keep growing and changing? What's wrong with not doing so?

4. Why are growth and change necessary in your marriage and in your other relationships? Think especially of your relationships with those who are younger than you.

Confusion

5. Describe a time of confusion in your life. What did you learn from it? What were the benefits of this time?

6. What kind of life events produce confusion? How does confusion affect others around you—family, coworkers, friends?

7. What part do calling and life message have in keeping confusion from derailing your life and purpose?

_____

_____

8. As the culture changes, what effect could it have on your thinking?

_____

_____

9. Review the keys to conquering confusion in chapter 16. How can these suggestions help you? Consider the disciples' reactions and the outcome in John 20–21 and Luke 24.

_____

_____

Withdrawal

10. Describe or define *withdrawal*. Does this relate more to men or women?

_____

_____

_____

11. Look at Jonah 1–2 and Psalm 139:7-12. Compare withdrawal and running away. What is the connection between withdrawing from people and withdrawing from God?

_____

_____

_____

12. Chapter 17 includes a list of possible antidotes to withdrawal. Pick one or two of them and describe how they have helped you in the past or could help you in the future.

_____

_____

13. What happens when you withdraw from relationships with others—your wife, family, coworkers, friends?

_____

_____

_____

Study 6

Chapter 18

You may not be in the fourth quarter of your life yet, but someday you will be. Certain dangers magnify themselves in this period. You may see many mistakes you've made in the first three quarters of your life. But the game of life isn't over yet. The fourth quarter allows you to recover from the past and rebuild. Also, all your achievements can be nullified by actions and decisions in the fourth quarter. If you aren't there yet, answer and discuss the questions as if you were.

Scripture Discovery: Read 1 Corinthians 9:24-27 and 1 John 2:12-14.

1. Everyone wants to finish life well, but not everyone does. What are some of the pitfalls you've observed in the fourth quarter of life?

_____

_____

_____

_____

2. Read and discuss the implications of the two passages above. How do they relate to the fourth quarter?

_____

_____

_____

_____

_____

3. How is a man's identity more or less obvious after age sixty than it was in the earlier part of his life? How does this affect your own thinking about your fourth quarter? To what degree have you already experienced a loss of identity or significance?

_____

_____

4. This is a good time to reflect on the previous "quarters" you've been through in life. List on a timeline the key defining events in your life so far (marriage, divorce, children, job successes and failures, mistakes, etc.).

_____

_____

5. How can your perception of your identity help you or hinder you? How does perceived identity or position either control you or humble you? How do you view yourself today in terms of your identity?

_____

_____

_____

6. How do you define _character_? How do you continue to develop your character now? Or is it fixed and unchangeable? How can it be damaged?

_____

_____

_____

7. Considering the four dangers of sin, withdrawal, freezing, and confusion, which one has challenged you the most? Why? How have you responded?

_____

_____

_____

8. How can you reform, continue, or develop your calling and purpose apart from work?

9. At the end of chapter 18, I suggest among other things the four actions or ideas listed below. Beside each one, write a sentence of how it could apply to you now.
   a. Surrender:

   b. Be generous:

   c. Be realistic:

   d. Be an encourager:

10. List and discuss active steps or strategies you can implement to make the fourth quarter the best part of your life.

11. Consider the following areas of your life. For each one, list and discuss something you can do to make it a better and more fulfilling part of your fourth quarter.
   a. Spiritual disciplines:

   b. Family:

   c. Marriage:

   d. Learning:

   e. Community (church or other):

12. What is one thing you have learned about yourself in this study?

_____

_____

Study 7

Chapter 19

We all want solutions to the issues we face in life. Usually, we want something we can do to get rapid results. We have faced and been challenged by many dangers. Some of these dangers may have plagued us for years. We would like some magic pill to cure everything instantly. That pill doesn't exist spiritually. Rather, we need to rebuild and renew the foundations of our lives. For men who've walked with God for a lifetime, you realize this renewal must be constant. As with diet and exercise, the effectiveness of spiritual renewal is demonstrated over time, requiring continual effort.

With this in mind, let's finish this journey with a focus on spiritual renewal. This will provide a foundation for handling all the dangers addressed in this book. We'll begin with spiritual renewal in the inner man.

Scripture Discovery: Read 1 Peter 1:1-15, Romans 7:21-25, 2 Corinthians 4:16-18, and Ephesians 3:14-19.

1. From the passages above, what do you observe about the inner man?

_____

_____

2. How would you describe the inner man?

_____

_____

3. What is spiritual renewal? Consider 2 Corinthians 4:16, Ephesians 4:23, and Colossians 3:10.

_____

_____

4. Where does renewal take place? How is your mind involved? Your heart and spirit?

5. Share a time when you experienced spiritual renewal. How did it come about? How can you discern when you need it again?

6. Discuss the concept of vitality.

7. Chapter 19 includes several suggestions to aid you in spiritual renewal (solitude, reflection, etc.). Which one is the most difficult for you?

8. How important is solitude? Where and how do you get it?

9. What's the role of fellowship and friendship in developing your inner life? Read Proverbs 27:9-10. Tell a story about when your friendship with someone spurred you to deepen your inner life.

10. What books have you read that stimulated your thinking about your inner life?

11. How does inner spiritual renewal relate to facing the dangers discussed in this book?

12. What do you need to do now to develop your inner spiritual person?

Study 8

Chapter 20

Thinking is not doing. Doing doesn't always come from thinking. All the spiritual renewal in your inner person must eventually reveal itself in what you do—in how you live your life. (This is a good point to debate.)

Scripture reading may involve meditation and memorization in order for it to sink in and produce change. Seeking solitude can require deliberate planning. Changing some of our habits will require discipline. You get the idea. But being and doing are intricately connected. Doing without inner motivation easily leads to legalism, and it soon results in dreary and empty activity.

Scripture Discovery: Read Galatians 5:16-23, Ephesians 4:25-32, and James 1:22-25 and 2:14-23.

1. What do these passages say about the outer person?

2. How do they connect inner renewal and our actions?

3. What happens when you have one without the other (inner renewal without outer renewal or outer renewal without inner renewal)?

4. Here are three phrases related to our responses to the Holy Spirit. How are they connected?
   a. *Grieve not* . . . (Ephesians 4:30)
   b. *Quench not* . . . (1 Thessalonians 5:19)
   c. *Keep in step with* . . . (Galatians 5:25)

5. What disciplines related to knowing the Scriptures are connected to the outer man?

6. What are some actions that are destructive? What are some actions that build up you and others for the better?

7. In this chapter, what did you learn about the Holy Spirit?

8. Where do accountability and fellowship fit in encouraging the outer man?

9. Since this is the last of these eight studies, it would be helpful to review the key lessons or concepts you've learned and to identify the most important takeaways from your reading, discussion, and application.

a. List four or five new truths you've discovered.

b. List two or three of your most impactful applications.

c. Which of the dangers challenged you the most, either in terms of knowledge or personal impact in your life?

d. What Bible passages helped you the most as you did these studies?

◆

This book and the companion Bible study and discussion guide treat only a small portion of the truth of Scripture and what constitutes living a godly and fruitful life. I trust that this will whet your appetite for discovering God's direction for you from His Word. The ideas and concepts of this book will never replace your digging into the Scriptures related to the many areas of your walk with God.

Now to him who is able to do immeasurably more than all we ask or imagine, according to his power that is at work within us.

EPHESIANS 3:20

About the Author

JERRY WHITE is the international president emeritus of The Navigators, a Christian ministry with more than 5,000 staff working in 112 countries, serving college students, military personnel, business and professional people, and churches.

He holds a BS in electrical engineering from the University of Washington, a master's degree in astronautics from the Air Force Institute of Technology, and a PhD in astronautics from Purdue University.

His thirteen years of active duty in the Air Force included an assignment as a mission controller at Cape Canaveral during the height of the American space program. He was also an associate professor of astronautics at the Air Force Academy in Colorado for six years and has coauthored a nationally recognized textbook on astrodynamics. He retired as a major general in the Air Force Reserve.

As a registered professional engineer, he's a member of the Tau Beta Pi, an engineering honor society, and an associate fellow of the American Institute of Aeronautics and Astronautics. In the early 1990s, he served as chairman of the Colorado Rhodes Scholarship Selection Committee.

Throughout his military career, he maintained close contact with The Navigators, helping launch Navigator ministries at the Air Force Academy and Purdue University. He served in several leadership roles with The Navigators, including president and general director.

He's an avid handball player, a licensed commercial pilot, and an active member of his local church. He has served on the boards of World Vision, Christian Leadership Alliance, Air and Space Forces Association, New Horizons Foundation, Evangelical Council for Financial Accountability, Greater Europe Mission, and the Lausanne Movement.

Jerry and his wife, Mary, have four children (the eldest, Steve, died in 1990), eleven grandchildren, and three great-grandchildren. They live in Colorado Springs.

His books include *Rules to Live By: 52 Principles for a Better Life*; *The Joseph Road: Choices That Determine Your Destiny*; *The Power of Commitment: How Ordinary People Can Make an Extraordinary Impact on the World*; *Honesty, Morality, and Conscience: Making Wise Choices in the Gray Areas of Life*; *The Church and the Parachurch: An Uneasy Marriage*; *Choosing Plan A in a Plan B World: Living Out the Lordship of Christ*. He coauthored *Fundamentals of Astrodynamics*. With Mary, he has coauthored *To Be a Friend: Building Deep and Lasting Relationships*; *Your Job: Survival or Satisfaction*; *The Christian in Mid Life*; and *Unfinished: How to Approach Life's Detours, Do-Overs, and Disappointments*.

Notes

CHAPTER 3: LOSS OF MOTIVATION

1. Stephanie Hertzenberg, "Phrases to Keep You Going When You Lose Motivation," *Beliefnet*, January 2022, https://www.beliefnet.com/inspiration /phrases-to-keep-you-going-when-you-lose-motivation.aspx?msclkid= eb102057bcff11ecb3d428fc100fb1c3.
2. Mary A. White, *Harsh Grief, Gentle Hope* (Colorado Springs, CO: NavPress, 1995).
3. Studs Terkel, *Working: People Talk about What They Do All Day and How They Feel about What They Do* (New York: The New Press, 1997).
4. John Piper, *Desiring God: Meditations of a Christian Hedonist* (Sisters, OR: Multnomah, 2003); Bob Goff, *Love Does: Discover a Secretly Incredible Life in an Ordinary World* (Nashville, TN: Thomas Nelson, 2012).
5. Larry Crabb, *Finding God* (Grand Rapids, MI: Zondervan, 1993), 174.
6. Elisabeth Elliot, ed., *The Journals of Jim Elliot* (Old Tappan, NJ: Revell, 1978), 174.

CHAPTER 7: LOSS OF CONFIDENCE

1. Louis L'Amour, "The Walking Drum," *Reader's Digest*, July 1995, 168.

CHAPTER 8: THE ANTIDOTE FOR LOSS

1. See a fuller discussion of this in Jerry White, *The Joseph Road: Choices That Determine Your Destiny* (Colorado Springs, CO: NavPress, 2009).
2. J. Oswald Sanders, *Spiritual Maturity: Principles of Spiritual Growth for Every Believer* (Chicago: Moody, 1962), 35–36. Emphasis added.
3. Sanders, *Spiritual Maturity*, 41.
4. Philip Yancey, *Where Is God When It Hurts?* (Grand Rapids, MI: Zondervan, 1977); Philip Yancey, *Disappointment with God: Three Questions No One Asks Aloud* (Grand Rapids, MI: Zondervan, 1988).

CHAPTER 10: WHEN SEXUAL TEMPTATION BECOMES SIN

1. Robert Hicks, *The Masculine Journey: Understanding the Six Stages of Manhood* (Colorado Springs, CO: NavPress, 1993), 65.
2. Hicks, *Masculine Journey*, 58, 69.
3. Jerry White, *Honesty, Morality, and Conscience: Making Wise Choices in the Gray Areas of Life* (Colorado Springs, CO: NavPress, 1996), 180.

4. Hicks, *Masculine Journey*, 65–66.
5. Robert Daniels, *The War Within: Gaining Victory in the Battle for Sexual Purity* (Wheaton, IL: Crossway, 1997).
6. Lonnie Berger, *Every Man a Warrior*, Books 1–3 (Colorado Springs, CO: NavPress, 2011).
7. Charles R. Swindoll, *Growing Strong in the Seasons of Life* (Grand Rapids, MI: Zondervan, 1994), 94–95.

CHAPTER 11: WHEN CONFLICT BECOMES SIN
1. Elliot Engel, "Of Male Bondage," *Newsweek*, June 21, 1982, 13.
2. Hicks, *Masculine Journey*, 76, 78.
3. Ken Sande, *The Peacemaker: A Biblical Guide to Resolving Personal Conflict*, 3rd ed. (Grand Rapids, MI: Baker, 2004); Ken Sande and Kevin Johnson, *Resolving Everyday Conflict* (Grand Rapids, MI: Baker, 2015).

CHAPTER 13: WHEN PRIDE BECOMES SIN
1. Oswald Chambers, *My Utmost for His Highest* (New York: Dodd, Mead & Co., 1935), daily reading for Jan. 12.
2. Alan E. Nelson, *Embracing Brokenness: How God Refines Us through Life's Disappointments* (Colorado Springs, CO: NavPress, 2016).
3. David Green, with Bill High, *Giving It All Away . . . and Getting It All Back Again: The Way of Living Generously* (Grand Rapids, MI: Zondervan, 2017).
4. Crabb, *Finding God*, 112.

CHAPTER 14: THE ANTIDOTE FOR SIN
1. C. S. Lewis, *Mere Christianity* (New York: Macmillan, 1960), 153.
2. Fred Hignell III, "Sharing the Paddle," *Moody Monthly*, July/August 1996, 51.
3. Patrick M. Morley, *The Man in the Mirror: Solving the 24 Problems Men Face* (Brentwood, TN: Wolgemuth & Hyatt, 1989), 274.
4. Morley, *Man in the Mirror*, 277.
5. Morley, *Man in the Mirror*, 280–88.

CHAPTER 15: THE DANGER OF FREEZING
1. Omar N. Bradley, "Armistice Day Address" (speech, Boston, MA, November 10, 1948), in Amy A. Kass and Leon R. Kass, eds., *The Meaning of Veterans Day: The American Calendar* (Washington, DC: What So Proudly We Hail, 2012), 11, https://www.hudson.org/content/researchattachments/attachment/1079/kass--themeaningofveteransday.pdf.
2. Winston Churchill in House of Commons Debate on the Address (November 4, 1952), Hansard Parliamentary Debates, vol. 507, cols. 7–134, https://api.parliament.uk/historic-hansard/commons/1952/nov/04/debate-on-the-address#S5CV0507P0_19521104_HOC_74.
3. Crabb, *Finding God*, 181.

NOTES

CHAPTER 16: THE DANGER OF CONFUSION

1. Gail Sheehy, *New Passages: Mapping Your Life across Time* (New York: Random House, 1995), 63.
2. Hicks, *Masculine Journey*, 174–75.
3. See White, *Joseph Road*.
4. Sheehy, *New Passages*, 243.
5. Sheehy, *New Passages*, 244.
6. Sheehy, *New Passages*, 271.
7. Chambers, *My Utmost*, daily readings for Oct. 23 and Aug. 1.

CHAPTER 17: THE DANGER OF WITHDRAWAL

1. Jan Johnson, *Enjoying the Presence of God: Discovering Intimacy with God in the Daily Rhythms of Life* (Colorado Springs, CO: NavPress, 1996), 8.
2. For information on conferences such as this, visit www.gleneyrie.org.
3. Richard Peace, *Spiritual Journaling: Recording Your Journey toward God* (Colorado Springs, CO: NavPress, 1995).
4. Jack Canfield and Mark Victor Hansen, *A Second Helping of Chicken Soup for the Soul* (Deerfield Beach, FL: Health Communications, 1995), 254–55.
5. Canfield and Hansen, *Second Helping*, 255.
6. Quoted in Canfield and Hansen, *Second Helping*, 280.

CHAPTER 18: THE FOURTH QUARTER

1. Chris Crowley and Henry S. Lodge, with Allan J. Hamilton, *Younger Next Year: Live Strong, Fit, and Sexy—Until You're 80 and Beyond*, 2nd ed. (New York: Workman, 2019), 266.
2. Greg Stephens, *Created for Greatness: Living Your Best Life through God's Word* (St. Paul, MN: Beavers Pond Press, 2020), 124–25.
3. Green, *Giving It All Away*.

CHAPTER 19: SPIRITUAL RENEWAL FOR THE INNER MAN

1. Henri J. M. Nouwen, *Making All Things New: An Invitation to the Spiritual Life* (San Francisco: Harper & Row, 1981), 23–24.
2. Nouwen, *Making All Things New*, 29.
3. A. W. Tozer, *The Pursuit of God* (Harrisburg, PA: Christian Publications, 1948), 69.
4. A. W. Tozer, *The Root of the Righteous* (Harrisburg, PA: Christian Publications, 1955), 56.

CHAPTER 20: SPIRITUAL RENEWAL FOR THE OUTER MAN

1. I'm indebted to Dr. Bruce Wilkinson of Walk Thru the Bible for stimulating my thinking in these areas.
2. Chambers, *My Utmost*, daily readings for Feb. 8 and Apr. 11.

NavPress is the book-publishing arm of The Navigators.

Since 1933, The Navigators has helped people around the world bring hope and purpose to others in college campuses, local churches, workplaces, neighborhoods, and hard-to-reach places all over the world, face-to-face and person-by-person in an approach we call Life-to-Life® discipleship. We have committed together to know Christ, make Him known, and help others do the same.®

Would you like to join this adventure of discipleship and disciplemaking?

- Take a Digital Discipleship Journey at **navigators.org/disciplemaking**.
- Get more discipleship and disciplemaking content at **thedisciplemaker.org**.
- Find your next book, Bible, or discipleship resource at **navpress.com**.

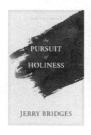

 @NavPressPublishing

 @NavPress

 @navpressbooks

CP1790